Storms, Fire, and Whispers

Hearing God through Life's Journey

By Rowe Stipe

DORRANCE
PUBLISHING CO
EST. 1920
PITTSBURGH, PENNSYLVANIA 15238

Dorrance Publishing Co
585 Alpha Drive
Pittsburgh, PA 15238
Visit our website at *www.dorrancebookstore.com*

ISBN: 978-1-6461-0768-1
eISBN: 978-1-6461-0033-0

Dedicated to Sid Ortis
and the Athletes in Action Ministry

Author Bio

Rowe Stipe was born and raised in Lafayette, Louisiana. He played baseball, basketball, and football from the time he was four years old, and lettered in all three at Ascension Episcopal High School. While he played basketball and football on and off, he played baseball every spring and every summer (and sometimes in the fall).

After high school, he played baseball at Hendrix College in Conway, Arkansas for four years until his eligibility was exhausted and his diploma received.

His summers were filled with baseball. Little League all-star tournaments when he was young, select ball and summer leagues when he was older. Once he got his driver's license he was on the road driving to summer league high school games, and to the tournaments when he was a member of the Louisiana All-Stars. While in college he played in the Red Stick Collegiate League and for the Acadiana Cane Cutters in the Texas Collegiate Baseball League.

He is currently a student at the LSU Paul M. Hebert Law School in Baton Rouge, Louisiana.

Foreword

"Insights"

I am honored to have been asked by Rowe Stipe to write the Foreword to this, his magnificent book!

As Rowe's Pediatrician and family friend, I have had the privilege of knowing him since he was born and it's been a great joy to be so closely involved in his life from the very beginning.

Rowe's parents, Mark and Jeigh Stipe, are our neighbors and some of our closest friends. Rowe and his sister, Mary Morgan Stipe, are not only our friends and friends of our children but also were my patients when they were younger. Over the past 27 years our families have lived closely through the ebb and flow of life, including childbirth, sports, school and social events, weekly "pancake nights", the coming and going of girlfriends and boyfriends, vacations, the ups and downs of (and graduations from) grade school, junior high, high school, college and professional school, birthdays, anniversaries, weddings, funerals and so much more. In fact, ours has been the epitome of life at its best (and, occasional, at its worst) all the while allowing us to experience God's many and abundant blessings!

Once, when Rowe was about 7 years old, I happened to be home at lunchtime on a weekday (a rare occurrence for me) when the doorbell rang. I answered the door and found Rowe standing there. Without hesitation he initiated, and completed, the following conversation:

Rowe: "Dr. Bryan, is Garrett home?"
         [Garrett is our son, who is 2 years older than Rowe]
Me: "No, Rowe, Garrett's in school today."
Rowe: "That's not possible; all the Catholic schools are off today." [Rowe and Garrett both attended Catholic schools, albeit different ones.]
Me: "Garrett's school is not off today."
Rowe: "Ascension School is off today."
Me: "Ascension is not a Catholic school."
Rowe: "What kind of school is it?"
Me: "It's an Episcopal school."
Rowe: "What is 'Episcopal'?"
Me: "It's a type of religion which isn't Catholic."

Rowe: "Oh" … "Dr. Bryan … "
Me: "Yes, Rowe?"
Rowe: "Do Episcopals pray to Mary?"

I share this with you not only because of its humor but also because it is one of many examples which demonstrates the incredible gift of insight with which God blessed Rowe and which was evident since he was very young.

This is important because, as I read through both the initial manuscript and the final version of this book, it occurred to me that one of the most salient aspects of Rowe's writing is, in fact, his unbelievable insight. His insight into scripture, his insight into life, and the application of his insight into the vicissitudes of his relatively short life, evoke memories of lessons I've learned from the writing of much older and much more seasoned theologians and authors.

Rowe was only 21 years old when he wrote most of this book … 21 years old! I can only imagine how much better the world would be if we ALL sought to maximize the use of our God-given talents the way Rowe has … and at such a young age!

It is my pleasure to commend *Storms, Fire, and Whispers: Hearing God through Life's Journey* to you and yours. As you read it, I am certain that you will share my joy of living through Rowe's thought-provoking life experiences and I am certain that you will be enlightened by the conclusions, life applications and recommendations he derives from these experiences.

Grace and Peace,
Bryan G. Sibley, MD, FAAP
Author, *God First - Setting Life's Priorities* (godfirst-thebook.com)
Certified Lay Minister, Louisiana Conference, United Methodist Church
Board Certified, General Pediatrics

Contents

How God Speaks to Us

*"He who listens to the Word will find good,
and happy is he who trusts in the Lord."*
                                    Proverbs 16:20

God talks to us in a lot of different ways. Some are obvious, some are subtle, some are loud, and some are quiet, but He finds ways to communicate with us all the time. You could be in the loudest stadium in the country and hear God as clearly as a conversation with a friend over breakfast.

Every once in a while, you may be dozing off in a meeting or in class when a light bulb goes off. Some people in history have had more dramatic experiences. People like Abraham, Moses, and Jesus' mother Mary have heard from God in loud, obvious ways. God sent an angel to tell Mary that she'd be the mother of Jesus and He talked to Moses in the form of a burning bush. For most of us, however,

God speaks to us inaudibly. We don't get large, flashing neon lights in the sky, but this doesn't mean that God is communicating with us any less; it just means that we have to hear Him in different ways.

Since the New Testament was originally written in Greek, it's worth looking at how the Greek language had a few different words to describe time. The word "chronos" referred to time in the context of history, and the word "kairos" was used to describe a specific moment in time. A "kairos moment" can describe a moment where we feel communication with God. Often times, this is when a thought suddenly pops into your head out of nowhere and you know it came from above.

This is very common. The frustrating part about it though is that it's hard to tell whether or not these thoughts come from God or from our own minds or emotions. Our human nature and our human mindset tend to distort or make us misinterpret what God is telling us. Luckily, God gives us a system of checks and balances. Whenever we feel as if God is talking to us, we can crack open God's word and do some research.

The best way to understand God is to get to know Him better, and the best way to get to know Him better is to learn more about Him and to talk to Him. It also doesn't hurt to surround ourselves with Godly people who can help us in our lives and help us grow in your faith.

Lean on these people in times of struggle because God put them in your life for a reason. The Lord uses these people to help, guide, and direct us in our own walks of faith. We never know how He will do it, but God always finds a way to get through to us.

Personally, in the last few years, for several different reasons, I've spent a lot of time driving all over the South. Hours would pass and the white lines in the middle of the road would start to blend together. Even though these drives were long, they were a great blessing because there has never been a time in my life when I had a better line of communication with Jesus. During those drives, I had a lot of time to think about a lot of different things from a lot of different topics, and I got to chat with God for hours at a time. A lot of these topics I thought about were completely random and had nothing to do with God at all.

I thought about everything under the sun, rehearsing conversations in my head, and worrying about things that would never end up happening. But between the road rage and internal dialogue, I felt like God used this time to communicate with me and to help me grow as a person. This seemed weird until I started to think about how God communicated with the people in the Bible in a variety of ways.

Sometimes He was dramatic like when he appeared to Saul on the road to Damascus or when he appeared to Moses in the form of a burning bush.

3

Other times, He spoke to people through prophets, and he even spoke through a booming voice in the sky when Jesus was baptized. However, most of the time God communicates with us or reveals Himself in non-obvious, often unexpected ways. A perfect example is the fact that God came to earth in the form of an infant, born in a manger, to a poor family.

Rather than coming down to earth with a grand parade of angels, God decided to reveal Himself to the world humbly. He did it this way because it takes a lot more faith to believe that Jesus is God when he comes from a poor family than it would if he came straight down from Heaven.

God does this a lot. If He was dramatic all the time, there would be no need for faith; so instead, God mostly talks to us in whispers rather than screams. Because of this, my time with God on the highway helped me grow in my faith more than any sermon ever could. And I think the biggest reason that I could spend time with God was because there was no one else in the car with me—I had to be quiet and just listen.

The best time to hear what God is saying to us is when we aren't saying anything. There's an old Sunday school saying that we were made with two ears and one mouth so that we listen twice as much as we talk. Fortunately, there are many ways that we can carve out time in our days to be alone with God. A lot of people get up early in the morning and read their Bibles and some like to go on hikes and be out in God's creation. It doesn't matter how, but having alone time with God is crucial. For me, it helped being able to spend hours at a time on the road, so I wrote down a lot of what I felt like God has taught me over the last few years driving from state to state.

Why Jesus?

"*Now, brothers and sisters, I want to remind you of the gospel I preached to you, which you received and on which you have taken your stand. By this gospel you are saved, if you hold firmly to the word I preached to you. Otherwise, you have believed in vain. For what I received I passed on to you as of first importance: that Christ died for our sins according to the Scriptures, that he was buried, that he was raised on the third day according to the Scriptures, and that he appeared to Cephas, and then to the Twelve. After that, he appeared to more than five hundred of the brothers and sisters at the same time, most of whom are still living, though some have fallen asleep. Then he appeared to James, then to all the apostles, and last of all he appeared to me also, as to one abnormally born."*

1 Corinthians 15:1-8

When you spend hours at a time staring through a car windshield or a bus window, a lot of thoughts come across your mind. With all of the traveling I've done in the last few years, because of baseball, I've had a lot of time to think about where my faith comes from. What would I say if someone asked me, "Why do you believe in Jesus?"

The reality is that everyone is betting their life on something. Whether you realize it or not, we're betting our entire lives on the things we each choose to believe in, regardless of whether or not these things are religious, because how we see the world, as well as the things we each care about are deeply impacted by our beliefs. If you think soccer is boring to watch, you probably wouldn't spend thousands of dollars to go to the World Cup. If you hate spending money, you probably won't buy a Rolex. Our beliefs determine our worldview. This is especially true when it comes to faith.

A Muslim will dedicate his life to the teachings of the Quran. If you're Jewish, you're betting that Jesus wasn't the son of God and was simply a rabbi who led a failed revolution against the romans. The same is true for every other religion in the world or the lack thereof. If you're an atheist, your betting your life that there is no god and that the universe came into existence on its own. But if you are a follower of Christ, you're betting your life and your eternity on the faith that Jesus was who He said He was. We're all betting our life on something, and there is a case for Jesus.

You don't have to be a comparative theologian with a Ph.D. to know that Christianity is unique from every other major religion in the world. While every other major religion was based on a history or text, Christianity is based on one event. Although we have a central text we go to in the Bible, the Christian faith wasn't founded on it. It was founded on the resurrection of Jesus.

The entire Bible could be seen as a roughly 4,000-year story about one bloodline. In the Old Testament, starting with Adam, there was a family lineage that included Abraham, Isaac, Jacob, then David, and then eventually, Jesus. The story of Christ was thousands of years in the making and culminated at the most important event in human history: the crucifixion.

When you think about it, Christianity should be the easiest faith in the world to disprove because the whole thing hinges on one event, so if you could disprove the resurrection, the whole thing collapses. But isn't interesting that after two thousand years, it's still standing? It's so simple to knock it down, but after 20 centuries, no one has been able to do it. And because of this, it's worth looking into.

We know through historical records that Jesus of Nazareth was a real man who lived in first century Judea and was tried, convicted, and executed by the Roman government. It isn't arguable that Jesus is one of the most documented human beings in history and that his death is likely the most discussed event in history. So we know that Jesus was a real person who was executed and buried, so the question isn't whether he was a real person. The question is whether He was who he said He was. He can really only be one of three things. Either He was insane and believed He was the Messiah but wasn't; He was a liar who pulled off the biggest scam of all time; or when He claimed to be God, He was telling the truth.

If Jesus wanted to scam everybody, He would've claimed a spiritual resurrection rather than a physical one because a spiritual resurrection would be impossible to verify or disprove, but instead He said that He would have a physical resurrection. So because Jesus publicly said that He was going to physically resurrect his body after being dead for three days, everything boils down to whether or not He walked out of that tomb.

If Jesus had never walked out of the tomb, there are only two things that could've happened. Either he was never resurrected or he never died in the first place. Let's look at both of these scenarios from the perspective of the Romans.

It would have been an absolute nightmare for the people in charge if Jesus were to rise from the dead. During the reign of the Roman Empire, there was a period known as the Pax Romana, which translates to "Roman Peace." It was a time when the Roman Government ruled with an iron fist and brutally stomped out any insurrection. This is when crucifixion came into play because they figured out that this was the most effective way to execute a criminal if you wanted to scare off any potential rebels. They would even have the crosses lined up on the road in and out of town so that everyone that passed through was innately warned about the consequences of taking on the Roman empire. So when the Jewish leaders came to Pontius Pilate and asked that Jesus be crucified, it wasn't a hard sell even though Pilate didn't think he was guilty of anything because it was his job, as the Roman governor of Judea, to prevent any potential uprising of the Jewish people.

So when Jesus was killed and then rumored to have risen from the dead, Pilate would've been faced with a massive problem. The guy whose execution he signed off on because of a potential uprising, was rumored to still be alive. This was bad news for Pilate; what could spark an uprising quicker than a resurrected revolutionary?

This was all to say that if it wasn't true and Jesus never actually walked out of the tomb, the Romans would have just presented His body and killed the Christ movement before it even started. If their whole objective was to prevent an uprising, why wouldn't they show everyone the body? If they knew it wasn't true, then what good would it do for them to go along with a lie that Jesus had risen from the dead?

Now let's talk about a different theory: Jesus walked out of the tomb because He was never dead in the first place. This is called the swoon theory and if you fall into this category, you aren't alone. The proponents of swoon theory usually believe that Jesus didn't die on the cross; He just passed out which would explain why He was able to walk out of the tomb.

Those who subscribe to this theory probably pass over the specifics in the crucifixion process, especially in the case of Jesus. It starts off by flogging the victim[1]; they take a whip with around a dozen leather strands and weave small objects into the ends of the strands such as ball bearings and blades, they then beat the victim a few times, usually no more than ten lashes depending on the criminal. However, when they did this to Jesus, they did it 39 times.[2]

---

[1] Mathew 27:26
[2] There was a belief in this time that if a person could withstand 40 lashes from a Roman flogging, then that person was immortal and couldn't possibly be a human. When they did it to Jesus, they stopped at 39 because they didn't want to have to face the reality that he was a god.

Some people have said that the damage was so brutal that the skin was completely ripped off Jesus's back and the muscle was exposed. They then made Him carry the cross through town and uphill to Golgotha[3] (think for a moment about how much of a pain it is to move a dresser or a couch, now imagine moving a ten-foot beam through town with no skin on your back). After they got Him to the hill, they laid Him down on the cross and pulled both of His arms out of the sockets, drove large spikes through His wrists and feet, then stood the cross up.

When the cross was set into the ground, His shoulders were set in a position to where it impossible to breathe. In order for Him to take a breath, He would've had to pull himself up with dislocated shoulders and then slowly let himself back down to exhale; this went on for several hours with His ripped-up back grinding against the wooden cross. After several hours had passed, the Roman guard put a spear through His side and out came blood and water, which we now know is a signal of death by asphyxiation[4].

The medical attention a person would need after all of that trauma in order to survive in a dark tomb for three days and then manage to roll a giant stone by himself isn't something He would have had access to. Due to the horrific nature of Christ's public

[3] Mathew 27:32
[4] *The Case for Christ*. IMDb, 2017. https://www.imdb.com/title/tt6113488/.

execution, it is impossible to reason that He could have avoided death on that hill. The question now involves the empty tomb.

If Jesus had never risen from the dead, then several things don't make sense. That would mean that the disciples were lying when they all wrote about seeing the risen Christ after the crucifixion. It would also mean that their ministries in the following decades were pointless, and every word written in the New Testament is a lie.

There's also the Paul problem. If Jesus was a fake, the case of the Apostle Paul is very strange. For starters, we know from biblical accounts that Saul of Tarsus, who later became the Apostle Paul, was a very successful man before his conversion. He sat on the Sanhedrin, which was the supreme court of ancient Israel and one of the most distinguished positions in the nation. He was wealthy. He came from the tribe of Benjamin, and in terms of his heritage, he couldn't have been more Jewish, a fact which made him despise the early Christian church. Saul of Tarsus hated the Christian church like Osama Bin Laden hated America.

It's not like his conversion was just another ordinary decision; it was anything but normal. Saul changing his name to Paul after becoming a Christian was a breaking news type of story. The weirdest part of the whole thing was that Paul claimed that the reason he changed his life was because he encountered Jesus on the road to Damascus long after Jesus had died. This makes Paul the most famous witness of the resurrected Jesus in history. Not only that, but Paul even went on to write most of the letters in the New Testament and became the greatest evangelist in history. He didn't just have a dramatic vision from God and then walk away like everything was normal. His entire life was fundamentally changed. So Paul either had a massive mental breakdown, or he really did see the resurrected Jesus.

The ministries of Paul and the other disciples also point to the resurrection. The disciples of Jesus gave up their lives for the Gospel, both figuratively and literally. We know that Paul, as well as the other followers of Jesus from both before and after the resurrection, didn't lead normal lives. They went from town to town and spoke to people about Jesus, often fleeing persecution from the Roman government. And at the end of their ministries, all of them, with the exception of John, were brutally killed. Matthew was stabbed in the back by a swordsman sent by King Hertacus. James was also executed with a sword. Phillip was scourged and crucified. Stephen was stoned to death, and Peter was crucified upside down by the emperor Nero. So not only did they dedicate their lives to Jesus but they also died for Him. This begs a serious question: if Jesus never resurrected and the disciples knew that

He never resurrected, why would they give their lives for something that the knew was a lie?

Some may say that religious fanatics give their lives for their beliefs all the time, but the reality is that religious fanatics die for things they believe to be true. This is the case for Islamic jihadists, the cults in the 1970s, and so forth. There are no cases that I can recall in which someone willingly dies a horrific death for something that they know is a lie. There are definitely no known cases where several people in a conspiracy die for a lie without one person breaking down and admitting that it wasn't true. It is highly improbable, even maybe impossible, that every single one of the early martyrs in the Christian faith died for an event that they knew never occurred. So because all of the disciples dedicated their lives to Jesus after He died and were all willing to be killed for their faith, their claim that Jesus did in fact raise from the dead has to be taken seriously.

The argument for Jesus is a topic that people have written entire books about. That case has been debated for two thousand years. There is also an equally valid case to be made about the uniqueness of following Jesus. From a doctrinal standpoint, the largest difference between Christianity and other religions in the world is that salvation doesn't come from a legal code but rather from a relationship.

The most common misconception in the world is that whether or not we can spend eternity with

God depends on our actions. In fact, the first eleven chapters of the book of Romans are an argument as to why that's not true. The only way of being saved is by giving your heart to Christ, and it doesn't matter what you have or haven't done up to that point in your life.

When Jesus talked about fulfilling the Law of Moses, He didn't mean that He was going to uphold a legal code, which would determine salvation; it meant that He would give us a better way of following it. Jesus didn't abolish the law; He set it on a higher level. For example, He said in Matthew that just by being angry at someone else makes us as guilty as someone who commits murder, and someone who looks at a woman lustfully is just as guilty as someone who commits adultery. He's telling us that all sin is equal in God's eyes. The only way to cleanse ourselves of sin is to give our hearts to Jesus and let Him do it for us.

To visualize this, imagine two branches: one that's full of leaves and just came off of the tree versus one that is just a stick. Think to yourself about which one is more dead. Most people would say that the stick is more dead because it has nothing on it while the other branch is vibrant, but the reality is that they're both dead because they've both been taken off of the tree. That's like us as human beings; it doesn't matter how good or bad of a person we may be because we're all sinners and need salvation.

The idea of complete and unconditional forgiveness is a radical concept compared to other faiths in the world. Aristotle, for example, talked about this unreachable divine realm above life on earth. In Greek mythology, that divine realm was on top of Mt. Olympus and in Norse mythology, it was Asgard. In the Old Testament, God exists in Heaven and in the tabernacle where our sin separates us from God.

This isn't the case with Christ; the divine for us is on earth. God saw sin and death on earth so He came down and confronted it by dying on the cross so that we could spend eternity with Him. In no other faith does this happen, and in no other religion does the creator of the universe come down to save humanity. Unlike Aristotle's view of the universe, God exists in the divine realm and here on earth. The Holy Spirit lives in the heart of each and every follower of Christ. That's an amazing part of following Jesus.

Following Christ is unlike any experience on earth; it's different. It's different because it's not what we deserve. Every human being is broken and needs a savior. Death comes for every man, but fortunately we serve a God who has beaten death. For followers of Christ, death isn't a conclusion; it's a transition point, where we get to be with God.

I won't deny that I am biased because of my faith. However, I will tell you that, when faced with the decision of whether or not to follow Christ, the choice could not be more obvious. Not only do we get to live a full life but we get to be with God once it's over. A life of following Jesus is unique because He is unique. The idea of a perfect and all-knowing God dying a horrible death just so He could be with us is an incredibly unique thing because it has only happened once.

Everyone who has heard about Jesus has to confront this question at some point: Why Jesus? Why should I dedicate my life to following Christ? The answers to questions like this lie in the uniqueness of the story of Jesus. The entire Christian faith depends on one man rising from the dead. It should be the easiest religion in the world to debunk, but here we are, two thousand years later, with more Christians on earth than ever before in human history. Jesus must have done something right. There is a tidal wave of evidence that He is real and that He died for us. He loves you so much that He gave his life for you knowing that you may never love him back. That's perfect love, and giving your heart to Christ is the best decision you could ever make.

Life to the Fullest

"*Therefore, Jesus said again, 'I tell you the truth, I am the gate for the sheep. All who came before me were thieves and robbers, but the sheep did not listen to them. I am the gate; whoever enters through me will be saved. He will come in and go out, and find pasture. The thief comes only to steal kill and destroy; I have come that they may have life, and have it to the full.'*"

John 10:7-10

In the fall semesters, due to the fact that we would be in the offseason for baseball, I would have the free time to go home one or two weekends. Usually, I would make those trips if LSU had a home game that weekend because night games in Tiger Stadium aren't events that you would want to miss, especially if it's a rivalry game. Between the atmosphere in the stadium and the tailgating before the game, LSU games are some of the most fun things on the planet. I would always drive back up to Arkansas the next day and wonder to myself if I was in the right place.

Those weekends at home, in Louisiana, were always so much fun. A big part of me was always reconsidering the life of a small-school athlete. Looking back on it now, I understand how ridiculous it was to consider leaving a great school where I had the privilege of playing baseball in order to have more fun at a bigger school. Even though the college life I didn't have may have seemed more interesting and entertaining, the college life that I did have in Arkansas gave me so many more opportunities to grow as a person in ways that I would have never thought of.

Jesus gave an analogy in John, Chapter 10 that related to this type of situation. To give some context, the Gospel of John is a little different from the other three. It was written a few decades after Matthew, Mark, and Luke because there was a movement among the early church that Jesus may have not been exactly who He said He claimed to be. There were rumors that some stories about Him were probably exaggerated, so John wrote his Gospel as a response to all of that.

In the Gospel of John, Jesus is a lot more straightforward with who He is. In Chapter 10, when Jesus gives the analogy of the shepherd, He's talking to

Jewish leaders, people that completely reject who Jesus claims to be. Jesus makes a claim here that we don't seem to believe nowadays. He says that if we come to Him, we can have life and have it to the full.

Normally, we tend to think the opposite: that a life following Jesus is boring and unappealing. A lot of times, people reject Jesus because of this. They don't understand His objective. They think that the Bible is just a giant rule book that will keep them from living their best life. When we think of Jesus as an annoying hall monitor who won't let us do anything fun, the idea of devoting our lives to Him isn't appealing at all.

The problem is that, sometimes, we don't see Jesus as a savior and a protector even though that's exactly who and what He is. He's often referred to as the "Good Shepherd" for two main reasons. The first is that a shepherd leads and protects his flock from people or animals that try to kill them, and the second is that if one of the sheep strays away, He'll drop everything to go track it down. In both cases, the reason why the shepherd does that is because sheep are very stubborn animals and they aren't that bright. They're a lot like humans. Just like the shepherd knows what's better for the sheep more than they do, Jesus knows what's best for us more so than we do.

The analogy that Jesus lays out in the passage at the beginning of the chapter is a little tough to think about, but notice how Jesus compares Himself to a gate. He doesn't say that the sheep run around aimlessly wherever they want; the sheep are in a fenced-in pasture. Sheep are domesticated animals and don't do well in the wild, so if the sheep wandered around wherever, they'd get mauled by wolves or other predators pretty quickly. But because they're safe and protected in the pasture, they can live a lot longer than if they had to live in the wild. The sheep may enjoy life outside of the pasture for a little bit, but then they'd have to contend with the forces of nature and they'd probably die because sheep aren't great fighters. However, the sheep that stay in the pasture are safe from those outside forces.

We're just like those sheep, and following Jesus is like deciding to go through the gate and into the pasture. Sure, the freedom of life outside the pasture and being able to do whatever we want is very attractive, but it also leads to death. In Hebrews, referring to Moses, it says, "He chose to be mistreated along with the people of God rather than to enjoy the pleasures of sin for a short time."[1] Sinning is a lot of fun, and if you say otherwise, you're lying or you didn't do it right. It's a lot of fun for a short period of time, but the hangover always comes.

The natural instinct of a sheep would be to go wherever and avoid captivity, just like our natural instinct is to do whatever feels good right now, but nature gives and takes away. The same short-term

---

[1] Hebrews 11:25

happiness we get from wandering off from God also comes back to bite us, just as the consequence of the sheep listening to its natural instincts would be death because it would get eaten. The same is true for us. The consequence of us listening to our human nature is death. Wandering off from the shepherd means we're going to be vulnerable to the forces of sin and death. When Jesus compares Himself to a gate, what He's saying is that if we live according to His will, it doesn't mean we can run around doing whatever we want, but it does mean that we can have life.

First and foremost, Jesus wants what's best for us, and the reason why He tells us to avoid certain things is because He knows what's better for us more than we do. The way the thief steals, kills, and destroys is by leading the sheep astray, and that's the same way that sin attempts to steal our joy and destroy our lives. It tries to lead us astray.

Sin makes the world away from Jesus seem appealing, but it's only after we hit rock bottom that we realize nothing in the world can truly fulfill us the way Jesus can. There simply isn't a substitute for someone who loves you so unconditionally that He'd forgive you for everything you did wrong and die for you knowing you may never love Him back.

There is nothing in the universe other than Jesus that can satisfy us the way Christ can. Everything else will eventually be gone, but the love of Jesus is eternal. Now, it may seem from this analogy that Jesus wants us to be prisoners, but His objective isn't to put us in a box and keep us away from everyone; He loves us way too much to keep us locked up. He wants us to have life to the fullest, and the reason why He does tell us to live a certain way is because He knows that it is the best way to live a truly happy life and that it's the only way to spend eternity with Him.

Sometimes we may think that we've simply made too many mistakes for Jesus to love us, or that we just aren't good enough to follow God. That couldn't be further from the truth.

In Matthew, Jesus gives another sheep analogy, except this time He compares himself to a shepherd rather than a gate. He talks about one sheep in a flock of 100 that wanders off, and the shepherd leaves the other 99 to find that one sheep. Every single one of us is like that sheep; we all wander off from Jesus at some point in our lives.

The interesting thing about that story is that Jesus never mentions how far the sheep wandered off or how long it took to track it down; it only mentions that it wandered off and that the shepherd dropped everything to bring him back. It doesn't matter how far you may have drifted away from Jesus or how long you've been away from Him; He loves you so much. Bringing you back to the flock is the most important thing imaginable to Him.

If you were the only human that ever lived, God would still die for you so you could spend an eternity with Him. In Romans it says, "While we were still sinners, Christ died for us."[2] The Bible even says that all of Heaven celebrates when one person decides to give their life to come home and give their life to Christ. Even though it may feel like the ways of the world are enough to satisfy us, the world will always let us down. Jesus never will; it's the reason why we can live life to the fullest if we decide to follow Him. Sure, a life with no rules sounds awesome, but there is always a price to pay. There is nothing out there that will give itself up for you the way Jesus did. There's nothing out there that cares about you they way Jesus does. Nothing we can ever do away from Jesus will ever compare to a life following Him.

There's also no in-between. Either we decide to give our lives to and follow Jesus or we don't. It's just like how that sheep can't be inside and outside of the pasture at the same time; it has to be one or the other. If you're currently facing this choice and you don't know if you're quite ready to follow Jesus or you're scared that a life after Christ won't be as exciting, just remember that God loves you more than you could possibly imagine, and He not only wants to spend eternity with you, but He wants you to have the best life you can.

---

[2] Romans 5:8

Not only is a life following Jesus not boring, it's the greatest adventure we could go on. Think about how much different the lives of some people would have been if they didn't make the decision to follow after God. Would David have killed Goliath? Would Paul be remembered as the greatest evangelist in history? Would Billy Graham have been able to fill stadiums? This doesn't mean that if you accept Jesus into your heart that you'll be a millionaire tomorrow, even though some pastors will tell you that.

Living life to the fullest means a certain kind of peace and security that washes over you and lets you know that anything in this life that could hurt you is only temporary and that the next life is infinitely better. Because of this peace and love, we can truly live life to the fullest.

Accepting Christ—The Bridge

"For the wages of sin is death, but the free gift of God is eternal life through Jesus Christ."

Romans 6:23

The greatest sermon I've ever heard happened on a beach in Gulf Shores, Alabama at sunset. It was during a training trip for a college athlete ministry called Athletes in Action, and as the sun went to its home in the western sky, with the crashing waves in the background, my friend Collin Radack picked up a bullhorn and started to address our group of exhausted college athletes at the end of a long, hard week.

Collin, being a natural leader, had this gift where he could inspire just about anybody. Normally, you would expect dozens of tired athletes in their early twenties to get distracted easily, but everyone was completely locked in during that cool May evening. He started talking about something called "the bridge". It's an illustration that he would use whenever he'd talk to someone about his faith, and because he was a baseball player, that conversation would usually happen with one of the young guys on the team in a one on one setting. So that night, he picked up a bullhorn and gave the speech that he's given a hundred times.

He started it off talking about how today Christianity is portrayed in two different ways.

Christianity A:
Salvation = Jesus + church + good works + reading your Bible + giving away money

Christianity B:
Jesus = salvation + we get to go to church + we get to read our Bibles + we get to give away money if we want to

Christianity A is nowhere in the Bible. A lot of times, religion will lead people to believe that in order to go to heaven, you have to give away a certain amount of money, go to confession, do good works, but that's not true. We've accepted the myth that anything we do on our own can help us earn or take away our salvation. If this were true, then Jesus' death and resurrection on the cross was simply for theatre and didn't mean anything.

Mankind is in a horrible position because we reject God regularly. We're all sinners. Romans 6:23 says, "For the wages of sin is death, but the gift of God is eternal life through Christ Jesus, Our Lord."

Now, the first eleven chapters of the book of Romans is Paul arguing that Jesus is the only way to Heaven: so, the death that Paul talks about here isn't a physical death, it's a spiritual one. He's saying that because we sin, we ultimately deserve to be eternally separated from God. Any sin, no matter how big or small, is a separation from God and disqualifies us from being with Him.

As a matter of fact, the term "sin" is actually an archery term, and it refers to the distance an arrow is away from a bullseye. So whether you're a quarter inch away or miss the whole target by eight feet, anything other than a bullseye is a sin. The same is true for us, whether you're a regular churchgoer or a serial killer, we've all fallen short of the glory of God and we all need saving.

Imagine trying to long jump over the Grand Canyon: you can train your whole life and be in perfect shape, but you wouldn't even come close to long jumping the Grand Canyon. Now imagine Usain Bolt or LeBron James trying it with you. Chances are they're a lot more athletic than you and would probably make it a lot farther than you, but none of you would even come close.

It's the same principle when it comes to our faith. If you were to think of the best person you know right now or someone like Mother Teresa, even if you would consider them a perfect person, they still don't even come close to a perfect, sinless life. We all fail right off the bat, which is pretty depressing when you think about it, but it doesn't have to be.

Rather than requiring us to live a perfect life and jump across the Grand Canyon, God built us a bridge when He sent Jesus. Right now, we're on the side of sin, death, anger, despair, and hopelessness and on the other side is God and peace. We don't deserve to be on the other side with God. We deserve to be on the side of sin because we're imperfect, but God chose to save us. He sent His son to die for us, so now, we don't have to be able to long jump over the Grand Canyon; we don't even have to come close. All we have to do is walk across that bridge. When Jesus died for us, He gave us the gift of eternal life; He gave us that bridge. So it doesn't matter if we continually fail. We don't have to be perfect; all we have to do is accept Christ and walk across that bridge.

A perfect example of this is in the book of Philemon; it's a one-chapter book in the back of the New Testament that probably takes up less than two pages in your Bible. The story goes that Paul is sitting in prison and makes friends with this other guy in prison named Onesimus, even though their crimes were very different. Paul was in there for preaching about Jesus and Onesimus was in there for running away when he had a debt to pay to his boss, who was a guy named Philemon.

In ancient Israel, when you owed a debt to someone and couldn't pay it back, you could work off your debt to the person that held it. The debt holder would pay for the debtor's living expenses, his food, give him a place to live, and he would support the debtor's family, and in return, the debtor would work off his debt to the debt holder. In this case, Onesimus had an obligation to work off his debt to Philemon but decided to run away because the debt was too big. Onesimus ended up getting caught and thrown in the same jail where Paul was being held. After getting to know him really well, Paul writes a letter to Philemon, which ends up becoming a book in the New Testament, where he offers to pay off the debt that Onesimus owed him so that Onesimus could be set free. He says, "So if you (Philemon) would consider me (Paul) a partner, welcome him as you would welcome me. If he has done you any wrong or owes you anything, charge it to me. I, Paul, am writing this with my own hand. I will pay it back…".[1]

---

[1] Philemon 1:18-19

Paul has no skin in the game here. He doesn't have any obligation to help out Onesimus; he could simply go on living his life and nothing would change for Paul. But instead of letting Onesimus rot in prison for the rest of his life, he pays off his debt. It's also reasonable to assume that it was a huge debt to pay because it was big enough for Onesimus to spend his entire life working it off, but without hesitation, Paul pays it off for him.

Every single one of us is in a situation similar to that of Onesimus. We all owe a debt that we can't pay: the debt for our sin. The penalty that Onesimus had to pay was a prison sentence, but the penalty that we faced was an eternity separated from God. But just how Paul paid off that debt so Onesimus could be free, Jesus paid off our debt by dying on the cross so that we can also be free. What's even better is the fact that we don't have to do anything other than accept that gift. Jesus stepped in and paid that debt off for us, but there is a catch.

Today, in the legal world, for something to be considered a gift, there has to be donative intent, meaning the person giving the gift has to intentionally give it away. There has to be delivery by the donor. Lastly, the person who receives the gift has to accept it. Two of those three have already been met. John 3:16 says, "For God so loved the world that He sent his only begotten Son so that whoever believes in Him will not perish but have eternal life." That verse shows that there was delivery because it says that God came to us. The New Testament tells us over and over that Jesus willingly died for us; there's the donative intent. The only thing left is acceptance. A gift is not a gift unless it's accepted. Legally, if your parents leave you an inheritance and you don't accept it, you don't have a right to it. It's the same thing with our inheritance from God. If we don't accept the gift of eternal life that He's given to us, then we don't have any right to it. It's amazing that the Gospel, a story 4,000 years in the making could be so simple: we sin and deserve to die, but Jesus died for us so we could spend eternity with God, and all we have to do to be free of sin is accept that gift.

That evening, sitting on the shore of the Gulf of Mexico, Collin Radack shared that message with us and then asked us a question: if you were to die right now, what are the chances that you would go to heaven? You could tell the whole group started to think about it deeply, and I remembered back to when he asked me that very same question in a restaurant, a year and a half earlier. At that time, when I was just a freshman, I thought, *Well, I've never done anything horrible and I go to church often, so I guess like 60-70%.* But he told me that the truth is, you're either 0 or 100%; there's no in-between. If there was an in-between that would mean that we could be saved through our works, which would also mean that there was no point in Jesus dying and that the Bible is wrong, which it isn't. Either we accept God's gift or we don't; we're either saved through faith in Jesus or we aren't.

Jesus gave us a gift that we don't deserve. The verse at the beginning of the chapter starts off with "for the wages of sin is death..." and because a wage is something we earn, it's telling us that we earned death. We deserve to be eternally separated from God. The amazing news of the Gospel is that we don't have to get what we deserve. The rest of that verse says "...but the free gift of God is eternal life through Jesus Christ our Lord." The beautiful thing about faith in Christ, which also separates it from every other major religion in the world, is that we don't have to live our life perfectly according to a code of laws to go to heaven. We just have to have faith in Jesus and accept the gift that He paid for with His death on the cross. If we do that, we can live our lives in freedom knowing that there's a better life waiting for us after this one.

On the baseball team at Hendrix, whenever we would reach out to our teammates about our faith, that's the story we would tell. We'd break down Romans 6:23 and share with them that we all deserve death, but because Jesus loved us, He paid that price for us so we didn't have to. On those long bus trips traveling to away games, I would sometimes look out the window and think about the impact that the

Gospel has had on the team. I would think about all of the guys who dedicated their lives to Christ as a result of playing at Hendrix, and how blessed I am to have been able to be a part of that team because I know that, without the guys on the team that lead me, I would have never fully understood what Jesus did for us.

I thank God all the time that He places us exactly where we're supposed to be, and, more than anything, I'm thankful that Jesus died in our place. If you're in a place right now where you want to make that decision for Christ but you don't know how, luckily Romans 10:9 gives us instructions.

It says, "If you confess with your mouth 'Jesus is Lord' and believe in your heart that He was raised from the dead, you will be saved." That's all it takes. All you have to do to accept God's gift to us is to believe in Jesus and to ask Him to come into your life. When you do that, you walk across the bridge.

A Lot Can Change in Seven Days

> *"Be patient, therefore, brothers, until the coming of the Lord. See how the farmer waits for the precious fruit of the earth, being patient about it, until it receives the early and the late rains. You also, be patient. Establish your hearts, for the coming of the Lord is at hand."*
>
> *James 5:7-8*

I've always loved to study the effective people from throughout history. It's fascinating to think about what they did to become successful. Specifically, I love to read about the great American military leaders in the past. People like George Washington, Ulysses S. Grant, Douglas McArthur, and most of all, George Patton. General Patton is one of my favorite people in history for a lot of reasons, but the story of his rescue of the 101st Airborne is easily my favorite.

Towards the end of World War II, when Adolf Hitler knew things were getting tough for him and Allied victory was on the horizon, he authorized an offensive with the intention of separating the American and British Forces. The plan was to move westward into Allied territory until they could get all the way through France. This ordeal later became known as the Battle of the Bulge. During this, the second most well known battle in World War II, General Tony McAuliffe and the 101st Airborne division marched into a Belgian town called Bastogne in order to control the seven highways that went through it.

Within a short amount of time, the 101st was completely surrounded by German troops. Things didn't look good for the 101st, and it looked like the only way to get out of that situation alive was for the Americans to wave the white flag.

But when the Nazis offered favorable terms to the Americans on a surrender, General McAuliffe responded by sending a note back to the Nazi commanders with one word on it: "nuts." Even the thought of surrendering to this band of barbarians was insane and unthinkable to the 101st. What ensued thereafter was a seven-day firefight between the 101st and the surrounding Germans. Meanwhile, George Patton, the commander of the 3rd Army, had paused his advance into Germany, turned around, and raced to Bastogne to liberate the 101st, but before he could get to them, he had to navigate through the Ardennes forest with heavy, armored vehicles, in a season with rough weather. When he and his third army were 30 miles south of Bastogne, Patton knelt down in a chapel in Luxembourg City and asked God for manageable weather in the last leg of their trip to that besieged city in Belgium. Soon after and miraculously, there were clear skies and General Patton was able to get to Bastogne and rescue the 101st airborne[1].

The fact that the weather was clear long enough for the third army to get to Bastogne was a miracle in and of itself. God gave George Patton that miracle so that Patton could be a miracle for the 101st airborne. From the time the fight at Bastogne began to the time where Patton liberated the city was seven days. For the men in the 101st, completely surrounded by the armies of a tyrannical nation, it must have been a long, desperate, and hopeless week.

Thanks to Albert Einstein, we know that time is relative. An hour spent eating dinner with your best friends would go by a lot quicker than an hour spent in a calculus class, so seven days on a honeymoon would be a lot easier and shorter than seven days in the besieged city of Bastogne. In a similar way, the times of adversity that we go through seem a lot

[1] OREILLY, BILL. *KILLING PATTON: the Strange Death of World War Ii s Most Audacious General*. S.l.: HOLT PAPERBACKS, 2019.

longer than the times in our life where God blesses us. Although life gets difficult, we serve a God that always comes through for us in His time. Often it feels like God is running late or that He abandoned us altogether, but that's never the case.

For the disciples, the days after Christ's death must have been but incredibly scary and traumatic. Not only did they witness their friend get executed in a brutal fashion, they also must have felt incredibly alone and abandoned because the man they had faith in to be a savior was gone. We can assume it was a rough weekend for them. But three days after that horrific event, God performed the most important miracle in the history of the world when Christ resurrected from the dead.

God's timing can be funny sometimes because He operates in a completely unpredictable way. The Israelites wandered in the dessert for forty years while waiting to go into the Promised Land, a trip that should have only lasted about two weeks. Before Jesus was born, there was a period called the "period of silence" when God didn't send any prophets to the Israelites and there were no books written for four hundred years. It was during this same timeframe that the Pharisees were able to rise to power and Israel was conquered by the Romans. Think about how exciting it would've been to be in Judea when the word started to spread that the Messiah had come after four hundred years of silence and thousands of years of anticipation.

God always comes through for us, but we may be at times in our lives where it doesn't feel like it. Maybe we're going through great adversity, facing what seems like impossible odds; we could be dealing with the loss or sickness of a loved one; we could have lost a job, and/or it could feel like our entire world is on fire around us. During these times in our lives, it definitely doesn't feel like a miracle is on its way. It could have even gotten to the point where you want to give up because you've constantly done the right thing but feel like life just keeps going backwards. You could be frustrated or feel stuck in sand while you see friends on Facebook getting married, having kids, going on dream vacations or getting promotions. Whatever we go through, always remember that no matter how dark the sky is, God is going to come through for us.

Now, the timing may not be what we expected. God might take a little longer than we want, but there is always a purpose for that. He always blesses us when we show patience and wait faithfully on Him.

Galatians 6:9 says, "Let us not grow weary in well doing, for in due season, you will reap if you do not give up." It's very possible that God will make us wait a while for that miracle, but it's also very possible that it could happen any day now. God could have easily sent Jesus in the fourth chapter of Genesis when the first sin is committed, but instead, He waited thousands of years to send the Messiah because He wanted the world to be in a certain place when He came. God may be waiting to perform a miracle in your life because He wants things to be a certain way when that happens.

At any rate, God fulfills His promise to us when He says, "I will never leave you nor forsake you."[2] It doesn't say that God will give us what we want immediately; it says that He will never leave us or forsake us, and there's a huge difference between the two. If we expect God to give us what we want when we want it, then we're essentially saying that we're just as qualified to make decisions as God is; that's clearly not true. As most of human history tells us, we make a lot of mistakes.

God, knowing how error-prone we are, doesn't always give us what we want when we want it because He knows the higher plan and we don't. So, when God promises us that He'll never leave us or forsake us, it means that life won't always be easy. In fact, most of the time following God involves walking down a harder path. More than anything, it means that we have to show faith and patience in the dark times that God is with us.

The phrase "never give up" might be the biggest cliché in the English language, and people offer it as advice all the time, but they never tell you how hard

---

[2] Deuteronomy 31:6

it can be to persevere. There has to have been a point during those 400 years of silence where some Israelites lost hope and thought a Messiah was never coming. The disciples must have felt lost, desperate, and hopeless when they saw their best friend be executed. Also, the men of the 101st Airborne must have wanted to give up when they were completely surrounded by the enemy.

Perseverance is hard because it requires us to push through adversity when the comfort of giving up is tempting, but we can't even entertain that thought. The moment we even think about how easy it would be to quit, it gets harder every second to keep going. Whenever we want to leave the fight or if everything seems hopeless and the sky is black, do one thing: wait seven days.

There is no guarantee that God will perform a miracle in our lives in seven days because He never goes by our timeline, but He will speak to us if we listen. Wait seven days and seek God in everything you do while constantly listening to what He's saying. A lot can change in a week, so whenever you want to give up, keep fighting for seven more days and then, at the end of those seven days, if you have to, stay in the fight for another seven days.

The Navy SEALs have what they call the 40% rule, which basically means that when you think you're done, you're only 40% of the way there. This is part of the mentality that lets them make it through hell on earth during SEAL training, and it's the part of the reason why they're able to be one of the most elite fighting units in the world and successfully perform some of the most impossible operations imaginable. The greatest people in history always persevered, and even though it may not seem like the current struggle is significant, we can honor God by fighting through it.

Within a span of a week, Jesus was arrested, tried, convicted, crucified, and resurrected. And then twenty centuries later, God sent George Patton to liberate the 101st Airborne after seven days of being pinned down by the Nazis. A lot can change in a week. Don't throw in the towel yet.

What to do in the Storm

"*Immediately Jesus made the disciples get into the boat and go on ahead of him to the other side, while he dismissed the crowd. After he had dismissed them, he went up on a mountainside by himself to pray. Later that night, he was there alone, and the boat was already a considerable distance from land, buffeted by the waves because the wind was against it. Shortly before dawn Jesus went out to them, walking on the lake. When the disciples saw him walking on the lake, they were terrified. 'It's a ghost,' they said, and cried out in fear. But Jesus immediately said to them: 'Take courage! It is I. Don't be afraid.' 'Lord, if it's you,' Peter replied, 'tell me to come to you on the water.' 'Come,' he said. Then Peter got down out of the boat, walked on the water and came toward Jesus. But when he saw the wind, he was afraid and, beginning to sink, cried out, 'Lord, save me!' Immediately Jesus reached out his hand and caught him. 'You of little faith,' he said, 'why did you doubt?' And when they climbed into the boat, the wind died down. Then those who were in the boat worshiped him, saying, 'Truly you are the Son of God.'"*

Matthew 14:22-33

In the fall of 2015, I had to make a difficult decision. When I was cut from the baseball team at Louisiana Tech, I had to decide whether or not to keep the dream alive. Was I supposed to transfer schools and give it another shot or was I supposed to stay put and just be a student? I had prayed for God to tell me what to do but really I had no intention of listening because I didn't think God would be concerned with my problems. I assumed that He had more important things to worry about than my baseball career; He seemed far away.

There was this feeling that God was more of a worldview than a father, and because of that I was starting to lose faith. But I'll never forget the day when that all changed. I was walking through campus and a random guy walked passed me with a shirt on that said "Don't give up." I thought that was kind of weird but just assumed it was a coincidence. Later on, I opened my Bible and the first page I saw had an essay, off in the margins that talked about never quitting. And then, about fifteen minutes after that, I talked to my high school coach on the phone and he told me the same thing he told me a hundred times: don't give up on something you love.

That day I could hear God telling me, in three different ways, to leave Louisiana Tech and try again at a smaller school, but that's all. He wasn't telling me where to go or how to get there. He seemed like more of a ghost who was talking to me than a savior who was walking with me.

I was scared to death. God was telling me to pick up and move schools just like that. I had to leave my friends and start the recruiting process all over again. Everything I planned for myself went out the window in the matter of two weeks. It was one of those moments where you feel like you're in the middle of the ocean trying to figure out what to do. Well, two thousand years ago, there was a moment like this with Jesus and the disciples.

The story takes place on the Sea of Galilee in first century Israel. What started as a thunderstorm is now one of the most legendary stories ever told. If Jesus had a greatest hits album, it would have the crucifixion, the resurrection, feeding the five thousand, and the time He walked on water. Sometimes, we even use this as a figure of speech to describe someone who is a great person; Randy Travis even wrote a song about his grandfather called "He Walked on Water." This is one of the most famous acts of Jesus, but there are a lot of things about this story that we miss.

This all goes down after another one of Jesus' most famous miracles—the time He fed five thousand men with five loaves of bread and two fishes. After He fed the crowd, He went up in the hills to be by himself and sent the disciples across the Sea of Galilee in a boat so He could meet up with them later. They left shore when it was early evening so they were going to have to be moving across the Sea of Galilee (which is essentially just a big lake) through the night.

While they were in the middle of the sea, a storm hit. Heavy rain started to fall, the wind started to whip pretty violently, and the waves started to get bigger and bigger. So here were the disciples, on this wooden boat, in the middle of the Sea of Galilee, at night, during a rainstorm. It's reasonable to assume that since these guys grew up in the dessert that they probably weren't great swimmers; maybe the ones who were fishermen could swim, but definitely not all of them. These guys were terrified. Everything that they thought could go wrong on this trip had gone wrong for them.

After a while, they started to notice something coming towards them, and at first they assumed it's a ghost. The Bible says, "Shortly before dawn Jesus went out to them, walking on the lake. When the disciples saw him walking on the lake, they were terrified. 'It's a ghost,' they said, and cried out in fear."[1]

As Christians, we do this all the time. We often make the mistake of thinking Jesus is a ghost. That sounds weird, but consider all of the times you had a problem, whether it was social, financial, athletic, medical, etc. and someone told you to pray about it and that sounded like impractical advice. I can't count the amount of times that someone told me to pray about a problem and I thought "yea, that's great, but what can I do to solve the problem right now?"

Often, even as Christians, we think of God as this far away being that we pray to for salvation, but when it comes to problems here on earth, He doesn't really help us. The reason I know this is because the disciples did the same thing. Earlier that afternoon, they saw Jesus feed five thousand people with one basket of food and here He is again, walking on water about to save them from this storm, and their first assumption is that Jesus is a ghost and not actually there. We do this all the time. During storms in our lives, when Jesus walks towards us, we think He's a ghost. We don't actually think that Jesus can pull us out of this situation, but this story tells us otherwise.

Right after the disciples started screaming because they were terrified, Jesus said to them "Take courage. It is I. Do not be afraid"[2] Then Peter tested

[1] Mathew 14:25-26
[2] Mathew 14:27

Jesus to make sure it was really Him. He said to Jesus, "Lord, if it's you...tell me to come on the water"[3] and then Jesus immediately told him to do it. I don't think Peter actually thought that was Jesus, and I genuinely think he was surprised when he figured out it actually was Jesus, and he was then even more surprised when Jesus told him to get out of the boat.

Think about this from Peter's perspective: you're in a boat, in the middle of this lake, there's this huge storm whipping the boat around, your best friend is walking on water, and then He tells you to step out of the boat in the middle of a thunderstorm; that's a lot to take in. The one thing separating Peter from drowning is this boat—it's the only thing keeping him alive. That boat is like our comfort zone.

When we ask God to bring us out of tough situations, He usually asks us to do something which requires us to step out of that comfort zone, and this is a very hard thing to do because we love our comfort zone. Like Peter, we may even think it's the only thing that's keeping us alive.

But here's the funny thing: do you think God didn't send that storm? Do you think Jesus couldn't have completely prevented that storm from happening in the first place? You may be going through a storm in your life, and God could have very well sent that storm so you would get out of your comfort

---

[3] Mathew 14:28

52

zone and trust in Him, which is exactly what Peter does. Right after Jesus tells Peter to come toward Him, he gets out of the boat and starts walking on water towards Jesus.

Whenever you trust God, get out of that comfort zone, and walk towards Him, He'll do something in your life that you never thought was possible. Moses would have never been able to lead the Israelites out of Egypt if he never left behind his quiet life in the dessert, and Peter would have never walked on water if he didn't trust Jesus enough to step out of the boat. In both cases, a miracle happened because of faith.

As inspiring as it is that Peter walked on water, what happens next is a cautionary tale. After Peter started walking on water, he started to look away from Jesus and instead started to get distracted by the wind. The Bible says, "But when he saw the wind, he was afraid, and beginning to sink, cried out 'Lord, Save me!' Immediately Jesus reached out his hand and caught him. 'You of little faith,' He said, 'why did you doubt?'"[4]

I pray we don't make the same mistake that Peter made. As he was in the middle of a miracle, he got distracted by his circumstances and took his eyes off of Jesus, causing him to start drowning. Either we are focused on Christ or we are focused on the waves. We can't give our attention to both.

---

[4] Mathew 14:31

If we stay focused on Christ throughout the storm, we get to become part of a miracle, but if we take our eyes off Jesus and try to go at it alone or we get distracted by our circumstances and lose faith, we'll drown. Fortunately, we serve a God who gives us grace instead of judgement. If we do get to the point where we take our focus off of Jesus and start to drown, He'll still save us.

Back in the Old Testament, Moses, like Peter, also had a tough time stepping out of his comfort zone. When Moses was called by God to go back to Egypt and save the Jewish people, he started telling God that he wasn't capable of leading the Jewish people out of Egypt because of his stutter. God's response was pretty straightforward. He basically told Moses that He was the one who created Moses with a stutter in the first place.

God created Moses with a speech problem knowing that someday he would be called to lead the Jewish people, and thousands of years later He sent the storm to the disciples. In both cases, God allowed adversity to happen so that faith would take over and a miracle could occur.

The adversity we face in our lives is there so that we can overcome it and glorify Christ. We just have to have the courage to trust Jesus and step out of the boat. If you do that, you have no idea the kinds of miracles that God can do in your life.

Faith Moving Mountains

"You don't have enough faith," Jesus told
them. "I tell you the truth, if you had faith
even as small as a mustard seed, you could
say to this mountain, 'Move from here to
there,' and it would move. Nothing would
be impossible."

Matthew 17:20

It's very easy to feel hopeless sometimes, especially
when we're alone. Every once in a while, I'll wake up
in the middle of the night and start to think of all
these problems that need to be solved, or I'll frustrat-
ingly try to plan out every detail of the future while
driving down Highway 167. Sometimes, we don't
want to know that faith can carry us out of tough situations because that would require us to give up control, and we don't want to give up control of the
steering wheel.

We naturally want to do things our way, but there are a lot of problems that we can't solve on our own. We could be at a point where we get overwhelmed trying to fix every issue on our own, or we could be in a position where we're waiting for God to show up. We all have things in our lives that we want God to resurrect.

It may be that you're in a period of life where your family isn't as close as it used to be; you may feel like life is passing you by; or you could be an athlete trying to come back from an injury. Regardless of what it may be, there are a lot of times where we're desperate for God to step in.

When I found out I wasn't going to make the team at Louisiana Tech, I felt like I was in limbo that entire fall. I was bored and I wanted nothing more than to get back into baseball again. I spent a good amount of time sending out emails to coaches at other schools asking them if they had a spot for me and I didn't get a lot of great feedback. I was getting very close to the point of admitting that my time on the field was over. Then, at the eleventh hour, I heard back from the head coach at Hendrix College.

I drove up to Arkansas and visited the campus a week later and made my decision to transfer there a week after that. When I first moved in that spring, I was scared and felt out of place. I couldn't avoid the thought that I had made a mistake, but as I look back on that time three years later I can see, clear as day, that God came through for me in a big way. I would have never been able to grow as a person and meet the people that I did if God had never taken my first school away from me. It scares me to think of all the blessings I would have missed out on if I was never led to Hendrix. God took a dead dream of playing college baseball and brought it back to life.

God has a tendency of coming through for us after we give up hope. In the second greatest comeback of all time, a man named Lazarus was raised from the dead by Jesus four days after he had died. But right before Jesus performed this miracle, Lazarus' sister Martha tells Jesus "...there is a bad odor, for he has been there for four days" and then He replied by saying "Did I not tell you that if you believed, you would see the glory of God."[1] And then, right after this, Lazarus walked out of the tomb.

We look back on this moment and think of how amazing of a scene this would've been, but imagine how stupid you would feel after this if you were Martha. Her friend Jesus, a guy she knew could work miracles, said He was going to resurrect her brother and she was worried about the smell. She's worried about something so insignificant that Jesus kind of ignores her comment.

The reason why Jesus wasn't worried about the smell is because He knew who He was and what He was about to do. If Martha had that kind of faith,

---

[1] John 39-40

she wouldn't have been worried about the smell either. Luckily for Martha, Jesus went ahead and resurrected Lazarus anyway, but there's a weird situation at play here. Mary and Martha, the sisters of Lazarus, were the ones who called for Jesus in the first place because they knew what He was capable of. They did show faith in Christ, just not at the last moment.

Sometimes it's scary to put our trust in Christ because we can't see him. When we're in a horrible position and we're desperate, it still takes faith to trust God with our situation, but it takes faith all the way through. Faith is a journey, not a moment. Mary and Martha called on Jesus when Lazarus had first died, but Martha doubted right before the tomb was opened. Fortunately, we get to serve a God who comes through for us even when we don't do the same for Him, but faith isn't a one-time thing. We're called to trust in Christ all the time, not just in our lowest points when we're desperate but also when we have something to lose.

Jesus tells us just how powerful faith can be. He says "For truly, I say to you, if you have faith like a grain of mustard seed, you will say to this mountain, 'Move from here to there,' and it will move, and nothing will be impossible for you."[2] Now, the reason why Jesus speaks with such strong language here is because He knows what

---

[2] Mathew 17:20

He is capable of. He's telling us that faith has nothing to do with our own abilities and has everything to do with God's.

Because Jesus is God, He is fully aware of what He did to bring the Jews out of Egypt and what He's about to do in terms of the resurrection. He knows that He can move mountains and He knows what a person is capable of if they were to put all of their faith in Christ. But notice that Jesus didn't say that if you have faith and you want the mountain to move, it will; He says that if you say to the mountain "move from here to there" it will move, because physically ordering a mountain to move involves action, and faith requires action from us. It does us no good to pray for something and then just sit there with our fingers crossed.

Another great example comes from the book of James. In one of the most famous verses in the New Testament, says "Faith by itself, if it is not accompanied by action, is dead."[3] This is a pretty bold statement, but it lays out the same principle that Jesus lays out with the mustard seed; real faith requires action. If a farmer desperately prays for rain during a drought and then prepares his fields for it, he demonstrates his faith in God to come through. On the other hand, if an injured person prays for recovery but never goes to the physical therapist, what good does he accomplish?

---

[3] James 2:17

There's an old joke about a Cajun man who prayed to win the lottery every month but it never happened, and eventually, he just gave up and stopped believing. Well, one day, he heard this loud booming voice from the sky, and asked, "Is that you God? If it is, I've been praying to win the lottery for years and nothing happens; do you just want me to be poor?" Then God answered back, in that same loud voice, "You have to meet me halfway; buy a lottery ticket."

James saying that faith without action is dead has two meanings. The first is that if we ask God for something but are unwilling to move in the direction He wants us to go, we won't reach our blessing. What good would the Founding Fathers have done if they prayed to be liberated from the British but refused to sign the declaration of independence or refused to fight the Revolutionary War? What about David? What would his legacy be if he never had the courage to face Goliath? When God calls us to do something, regardless of how daunting it may be, we have to have the courage to have faith.

The second point that James made is that following Christ also involves striving to live like Him. The whole point of Jesus dying for us was that it doesn't matter how messed up we are or how many mistakes we've made; we can still spend eternity with God. Doing good works is not what gets us saved, but it's a pretty good signal that our hearts have changed.

God gives us the same promise that he gave Ezekiel; He says, "I will give you a new heart and put a new spirit in you. I will remove from you your heart of stone and give you a heart of flesh." When we give our lives to Christ, He gives us a new heart, and that new heart comes with the faith of following Jesus. By no means is the Bible saying that we can't be saved if we accept Jesus but don't do any good works. It's saying that the signal that we've given our life to Jesus is that change of heart and that longing to do good things.

A lot of times when Jesus was confronted by the Pharisees regarding the law, His answer always followed on the same theme: He would talk about the heart in some way. When He tackled the question of murder, He said that if you're angry at your brother, you're guilty of murder. When the Pharisees accused the woman of adultery, Jesus forgave the woman instead of condemning her. He knew that all murders stem from anger and that this woman's adultery stemmed from her not being loved the way that she should've, so He changed the objective.

He tells us to fix our hearts because if we truly love our neighbors, we won't ever murder them, and forgiving someone is a much more effective way of helping them grow as a person than condemning them. So that verse in James is taking this concept and putting it a different way: our faith in Jesus will make us want to do good works because our heart is changed.

Lastly, one of the major messages of the parable of the mustard seed is that you have no idea what you're capable of if you surrendered everything to Jesus and had the faith to walk in His direction. Sometimes, we just have to have the courage to go when God tells us to go and to stop when God tells us to stop. Faith the size of a mustard seed can move mountains, but we need action; we need the courage to tell that mountain to move. We need the courage to change and to move forward if we're ever going to get to the blessing that God has for us.

Faith, Hope, and Love

"If I speak in the tongues of men and of angels, but have not love, I am a noisy gong or a clanging cymbal. And if I have prophetic powers, and understand all mysteries and all knowledge, and if I have all faith, so as to remove mountains, but have not love, I am nothing. If I give away all I have, and if I deliver up my body to be burned, but have not love, I gain nothing. Love is patient and kind; love does not envy or boast; it is not arrogant or rude. It does not insist on its own way; it is not irritable or resentful; it does not rejoice at wrongdoing, but rejoices with the truth. Love bears all things, believes all things, hopes all things, endures all things. Love never ends. As for prophecies, they will pass away; as for tongues, they will *cease; as for knowledge, it will pass away. For we know in part and we prophesy in part, but when the perfect comes, the partial will pass away. When I was a child, I spoke like a child, I thought like a child, I reasoned like a child. When I became a man, I gave up childish ways. For now we see in a mirror dimly, but then face to face. Now I know in part; then I shall know fully, even as I have been fully known. So now faith, hope, and love abide, these three; but the greatest of these is love."*

1 Corinthians 13: 2-13

One weekend during the summer, the team bus had gotten back to the field after an away game at around 5:00 am. Now, when you're driving home at 5:00 in the morning after being on a bus for six and a half hours with 25 other guys who haven't showered in a day, you start to evaluate the direction of your life. I started thinking about how much I loved baseball and why that love for the game causes people to dedicate so much of their lives to it. This then made me think about why love is so powerful. Naturally, the famous passage that is commonly read at weddings came to mind: 1 Corinthians 13.

In today's culture, we have a warped view of love. We tend to see love as a type of emotion. We see love as a noun and not as a verb. Regardless of how we look at it, it's clear that we currently live in a world absent of love in a lot of places. According to the American Psychological Association, somewhere between 40%-50% of marriages end in divorce[1] compared to 21% sixty years ago,[2] but it doesn't just stretch into marriage; in a poll done by the New York Post in October 2017, 70% of Americans believed that, as a nation, we're more divided than we were during the Vietnam War.[3] It's clear that we live in an angry world, and we need real love as soon as possible.

Pop culture today also has a tendency to misrepresent what love is. It tends to present love as a type of infatuation, but it isn't. At this point, a lot of us are like the lyrics of a Foreigner song; we want to know what love is. If this is you, look no further than Jesus. He submitted to the worst pain anyone has ever felt and suffered an undeserved death so that we could have the chance to spend eternity with Him. Not to mention that He did all of this knowing that we may never love Him back; that's what perfect love looks like.

If that sounds too pie-in-the-sky and you want a more practical definition, check out 1 Corinthians 13, the most popular scripture passage to read at weddings. The chapter basically gives a checklist of

---

[1] http://www.apa.org/topics/divorce/
[2] https://divorce.lovetoknow.com/Historical_Divorce_Rate_ Statistics
[3] https://nypost.com/2017/10/28/america-is-most-divided-since-vietnam-war-poll/

what perfect love looks like: it's patient, kind, humble, selfless, and most of all, durable, meaning it never goes away or fails.

When Paul wrote 1 Corinthians, the church in Corinth was starting to fall into bad habits and there was a lot of division in the church, and 1 Corinthians also was written during the reign of the Emperor Nero who was thought to be one of the most brutal dictators who ever lived. They were definitely living in an angry time, so when Paul wrote this, it was to an audience that desperately needed to be reminded what love looked like.

The interesting thing about 1 Corinthians 13 is that you can replace the word "Love" with "God" and it still makes sense. The first three verses talk about how important love is and how anything we do without love will eventually fade away and mean nothing, the next five verses describe perfect love, and then the end of the chapter describes how everything that isn't love doesn't last. Isn't this the perfect description of God?

If we build up massive fortunes and become world famous but don't have a relationship with God or someone to share it with, in the scope of eternity, anything we earn will be meaningless if we can't help lead people to Christ and do good for the world. There's that old saying, "when you're on your death bed, you won't regret not spending enough time at the office," because in life, the most important things are free. Over time, generational wealth goes away; trophies collect dust; and stuff goes out of style.

The things we obsess over don't last, but love does and so does God. The love that we have for the people in our lives is more important than any amount of cash. And more so, our relationship with Christ is more important than anything else because it never goes away and it never fails.

The second section of the chapter also describes both love and God. Both are patient, kind, selfless, humble, forgiving, and neither one will ever fail or die. Money is gained and lost every single minute of the week, but love is forever. Both the love we have for the people close to us and the love we have for Christ are more important than anything else this world has to offer. Not only does love endure, but a lot of times, we find that things not built on love collapse.

Every year, the Federal Reserve performs "stress tests" on banks with more than $10 billion in assets. They take all of the bank's information, put it into a computer, and simulate different environments to see how the bank would perform under adverse economic conditions. They do this to make sure that bank wouldn't fold if a recession were to hit.

If we apply the same types of tests to relationships, we'll find that the relationships based on emotion will fold and the ones based on principle can withstand hard times.

As a perfect example: *The Bachelor* is one of the most popular shows on television and it's been running for over twenty seasons. After all of those couples that got started on that show, only one is still together as of the summer of 2018.

Anyone can start a relationship in a perfect, emotional environment manufactured by Hollywood, but those types of relationships can't make it through difficult periods. By the way, this doesn't just apply to romantic relationships; it applies to friendships also. Anyone can be buddies at a country club, but when you're stuck on the side of the road late at night in 30° weather, your buddy won't get out of bed to help you, but your friend will.

The difference between being buddies and being friends is love. At different stages of your life you'll be close to some people simply because they're around you regularly, but a close friend is there for you even when the two of you are thousands of miles apart from each other because love bears all things, endures all things, and it never fails.

In the Gospel of Matthew, Jesus gives a parable of a house built on sand vs. a house built on rock. When the storm came, the house built on sand was destroyed while the house built on rock was still standing. The question isn't if a storm comes, it's when. And when the storm comes, we find out that the relationships built on emotion will collapse and the ones built on love will ride it out.

If you're in a situation right now, after reading this, where you're not sure how some people in your life stand with you, or if you aren't sure whether or not there's love in that relationship, ask yourself: is there patience, kindness, humility, and selflessness here? Will this friendship or relationship bear, believe, hope, and endure all things? Nothing can come close to the glory of God, and nothing can ever come close to the perfect love that Christ shows for us, but the sign of real love in a fallen world is effort. Do you and your friend/wife/ husband/relative make an effort to show this kind of love to one another?

If so, then you're on the right track. We're called to love each other as Christ loved us, and although this may be an impossible task, making the effort to do so is not, just like how it's an impossible task to be like Jesus, but striving to do so leads to incredible things.

1 Corinthians 13 ends with the sentence, "*So now faith, hope, and love abide, these three; but the greatest of these is love.*" Why would Paul tell the church in Corinth that love is more important than hope and faith? It's weird to think that the Bible would rank these, but not when you consider eternity. In heaven, because you're with God, there's no need for faith. Hebrews says that "faith is confidence in what we hope for and assurance about what we do not see."[4] Faith is all about trusting

---

[4] Hebrews 11:1

God when we can't see Him or what the future holds, but in Heaven, God is visible and there is no future, so faith doesn't exist in Heaven.

Hope is knowing that things will get better regardless of how bad the world may be right now, and it also means knowing that Christ will come back one day and get rid of all evil in the world. But the same thing is true for hope that is true for faith; when we get to heaven, there's no need for hope because we'll already be with God. There won't be anything more we could possibly ever need or want.

Love, however, will live on for all of eternity because the love God has for us will never go away. It's always been there and it will always be there; that's why it's greater than faith and hope, and that's why love ultimately is what can save the world.

Feared or Loved

"There is no fear in love, but perfect love casts out fear. For fear has to do with punishment, and whoever fears has not been perfected in love."

1 John 4:18

The Office is one of the greatest TV shows of all time; it's made millions of people laugh since 2005 when it came out. In one of the most quotable lines from all nine seasons, Michael Scott says, "Would I rather be feared or loved? Easy, I want people to be afraid of how much they love me." Now, even though that's a joke, it does bring up a deep, philosophical question: would you rather be feared or loved?

It's tough to answer because people can be influenced by either one. If everyone is afraid of you, then they'll do what you tell them to because they don't want you to hurt them.

On the other hand, if everyone loves you, people will listen to what you have to say and will be more open to advice you give them or favors you ask of them. So if we can influence people with either one, the question really comes down to what kind of influence you want to have: positive or negative.

If you want everyone to be afraid of you, then you don't really care about what they think of you, you just care about the direction you're going. And if you want everyone to love you, you'd be more concerned with the impact you have on others. So would you rather be feared or loved?

The key difference between the two is that fear is a natural emotion and love isn't. Fear is rational and love is irrational. Humans have a natural ability to recognize danger and respond to it by either running from it or fighting it head on, which is called the fight or flight instinct. This is why we have adrenaline rushes; it's our body naturally responding to danger. In prehistoric times, people had to worry about predators like saber tooth tigers,[1] and throughout history we've evolved dealing with different problems. Yet we're still here; we aren't extinct. And not only that, but we're thriving as a species.

So in the long run, it seems like fear doesn't really stop us. However, unlike fear, love isn't natural and it isn't rational; it comes from a higher place. Love doesn't have the same limitations as fear be-

---

[1] https://source.wustl.edu/2005/02/early-humans-were-prey-not-killers/

cause it comes from God, not from nature. It's more powerful than any emotion we could have, including fear. The Gospel of John even tells us that not only is love greater than fear but that love also casts out fear.

The reason why bullies lose and dictators get overthrown is that eventually, people get to a level of desperation or they hit their boiling point, and when that happens, they forget fear and take on the bully. A perfect example is the American Revolution. The colonies had gotten to a point where they weren't going to tolerate the crown anymore and decided to form a new nation. Their longing for freedom was bigger than their fear of the British government.

Love on the other hand is a lot more durable; no one gets fed up with love and it has the power to influence people in a positive way that is much more effective than fear.

At the end of the day, love is the most powerful thing in the world. It's so important that the Bible says that God is love. It doesn't say that God has love, it says that He is love; it's who and what He is. Love is the greatest thing about life, but we've managed to get it wrong lately. We tend to see love only on the emotional level. Love is more than the butterflies-in-the-stomach feeling; it's about how we treat another person. It means putting that person before ourselves.

In the Greek language, there were three words for love, each with a different meaning: *Phillia, Eros,* and *Agape. Eros* referred to romantic love. *Phillia* is about the type of love between friends; this is where Philadelphia, the "city of brotherly love," gets its name. *Agape* is the unconditional, perfect love, like the love that God has for us.

The reason that the Greeks had three different words for love is because they understood how complicated it was and how it can take on several different forms. They knew that the love you have for your spouse is very different than the love you have for your best friend or the love you have for your child. The Bible also understands this but whenever it talks about love, it talks about it with the same central theme: love is selfless. The Gospel of John gives us a definition of what ultimate love looks like; it says, "Greater love has no one than this, to lay down one's life for one's friends."[2]

Even though Jesus understands that love has a lot of different layers, He tells us that at every level, truly loving someone means being ready to give up our own lives for them.

Love is complicated because it takes on many forms, but at the same time, it's incredibly simple. It means putting others ahead of ourselves. Whenever two people get married, they give up their old lives as individuals and become one. When you have

---

[2] John 15:13

a child, he or she is now your biggest responsibility, and your primary purpose in life is to give that child the best life you can.

Rather than human nature, which tells us to get as much as we can for as little effort, love tells us to do the opposite. It tells us to constantly make ourselves secondary. It's so powerful that it overrides our natural instincts. It's the only thing in the world that can make you give up half of your stuff when you get married, paint your face when football season comes around, and get out of bed at 2:15 am when your friend needs a ride home.

Unfortunately, as great as love is, it can lead to pain. You may love someone and they don't love you back, you may have been dumped before, or someone close to you may have passed away. After those things happen, we naturally want to shut down and close off our hearts to protect ourselves from getting hurt again. Our human nature takes over and kicks out love.

Jesus even talks about this in the Parable of the Sower. He uses seeds being thrown in a field as an analogy for hearing the Gospel. The seeds land in one of four spots: rocky soil; surrounded by thorns; good soil; or on the path.[3] The reason why the seed falling on the path was a bad thing is because the pathways through the fields would be walked on by the farmers so much that the dirt would pack in tight and nothing could grow on it.

---

[3] Mathew 13:3-9

When Jesus mentioned seeds falling on the pathway, He was talking about the people whose hearts have been walked on so much that it's tough for them to receive Jesus because it's tough for them to open up to something. Jesus understood that people who have been hurt will naturally want to protect themselves and will be less likely to love. And while it is true that if we never loved anything or anyone, we would never get hurt, it's also true that we'd live a horrible life if we did that.

It's kind of like finance: if we're so scared of a bad investment that we never invest in anything, we'd never make money. In the short run, it's very difficult to have an open heart after something bad happens, but in the long run, it strengthens our ability to love even more.

It's a lot easier to understand love by thinking about God and vice versa. Sometimes, God tells us no or lets us face adversity so that we can be stronger, and the same is true about love. Every once in a while, we can get hurt, but if we don't close off our hearts, we become better because of it. The Bible says that love is greater than faith and hope. It also says that love never fails. It never fails because it's the greatest and most powerful thing about life. It's more powerful than fear, financial problems, injuries, hard times, and death. And most importantly, love is more powerful than death. When Jesus died and rose again for us, He beat death. His perfect love for us was more powerful than the grave, and it still is today.

Let love motivate you more so than fear, money, or anything else. If you're in pain right now because you loved someone and they're now gone, don't let that pain get the better of you and keep you from experiencing the best part of life. On the other hand, if you're in a great place right now, don't let the love you feel go away when things get tough. Always understand that love never fails because it comes from God. Even Jesus went through pain when He was beaten and crucified, but that pain didn't last and fear wasn't enough to stop Him. His love for us earned the victory when He walked out of the tomb two days later. Tough times will come and go, so take joy in the fact that love is undefeated.

History's Greatest Hero

"'I am the Alpha and the Omega' says the Lord God, 'who is, and was, and is to come, the Almighty'"

- Revelation 1:8

I had a friend in college that spent the summer before his senior year doing mission work in India. He was one of the first people I talked to after we all drove in for the semester, so naturally, the first thing I asked him about was his mission trip. He told me that he and his group would wake up every day and go door to door telling people about Jesus. It meant the world to him and to the people he was spreading the Gospel to. When I asked him what his biggest takeaway from his mission trip was and he told me, "I learned that people are generally the same."

At first, I was a little confused by that answer until he explained it to me. He basically told me that even though people grow up in different parts of the world, human nature stays the same, even though there are different problems that people face. A bad day for us in America may involve getting fired. A bad day for someone in Syria right now may involve their whole family being killed. Even though the problems others face can be horribly different from our own, generally, we all deal with mistakes we've made in the past, try to do our best in the present, and worry about the future.

Part of being human also means facing the reality that the world isn't perfect. We've understood that life involves challenge. And because of this, even going back to some of the earliest civilizations, humans have always been infatuated with the idea of a hero: someone that comes in and fights the battles that we can't win. Just like the ancient Greeks told stories about Hercules, nowadays, we also love the story about Luke Skywalker when he leaves the family farm, becomes something more than the average man, and helps take down the empire. Whether it's *Star Wars* or *The Illiad*, people throughout history love hearing about a hero.

This consistency in storytelling from the ancient world until now begs the question: why do humans find the concept of a hero so interesting? Could it be possible that humans evolved knowing that life was difficult and that we all need help at times? We know that humans, even since prehistoric times, have moved together in packs to survive, and even now people tend to flock to other people. Every day, people move to big cities with huge populations or the suburban areas around them. Since the beginning of time, humans have understood that life isn't as difficult when there are other people around you who can compliment your skill set and help you with the things you struggle with; hunters traveled with gatherers, and salesmen work with developers. And so the concept of a hero, someone who is the ultimate helper, has always been attractive to people because we've understood our own weaknesses and how flawed we are, and I think that's by design.

In the book of John, Jesus talks a lot about how much we need him; verse 15:5 says, "I am the vine; you are the branches. Whoever abides in me and I in him, he it is that bears much fruit, for apart from me you can do nothing."[1] And then later on, he says, "This is the bread that comes down from heaven, so that one may eat of it and not die. I am the living bread that came down from heaven. If anyone eats of this bread, he will live forever."[2]. Jesus is clearly telling everyone that we can't truly live without Him, and it's not only in the book of John that we see this. When God gives the ten commandments, in the first one, He says, "I am the Lord your God, who brought you out of Egypt, who

---

[1] John 15:5
[2] John 6:50-71

brought you out of the house of slavery. You shall have no other gods before me."[3]

He makes it very clear that He's the reason that the Israelites have their freedom. In the first eleven chapters of Romans where Paul talks about how it's impossible to get to heaven on our own. All through the Bible God lets us know time and time again that we can't do things on our own and that we need Him.

The Bible itself is a story from the beginning of time, through Jesus' resurrection, and ends with the early Christian church. The whole thing is one giant hero story—the kind we learn about in high school English class. It starts with the status quo in the Garden of Eden, which doesn't last long; then they sin and humanity falls, which was the call to action. The rising action is the long story of the Israelites and Jesus' ministry; the climax is the resurrection; the falling action is the everything after the resurrection, including present day, and the new status quo will be the day when Christ comes back and destroys evil.

We're a part of the greatest story ever told. All of human history happens at some stage of Christ's journey, and so it's no coincidence that we're conditioned to be obsessed with the hero story. It's also not by chance that people naturally need each other; we need help with whatever we do. We've fallen in love with the hero story because it mimics our need for Christ.

---

[3] Exodus 20:2-3

When the Greeks told each other the legends of Hercules; they did it because they loved hearing about a hero who could overcome the monsters around them. Every ancient civilization had their own hero stories as well as their own accounts of how the universe came to be, what happens after we die, and what's going to happen at the end of time. It's because, all throughout the history of the world, people have found themselves in a mysteriously orderly and unjust world. And because of this, people have always been curious about why the world is orderly and hopeful that justice will ultimately prevail.

All of these human traits are like puzzle pieces that work us into the greatest story ever told. The reason why *The Avengers* or any movie about Navy SEALs grosses millions of dollars of revenue at the box office is because we love seeing movies about heroes who can become more than the average man and overcome extraordinary evil. We love to be reassured that no matter how big the battle ahead of us may be or regardless of how daunting our current enemy is, good will always triumph over evil in the end because that's the ultimate story of the universe. Eventually there's going to be a day when Christ comes back and rescues the world from evil and darkness.

There are two major positives we can take from this. The first is that we can have a sense of purpose; we know that our lives aren't pointless. We aren't on this earth just to take up space and breathe oxygen for a few decades. We get to play a role in the greatest fight in history: the war between good and evil. We have to understand that God created us exactly the way each of us are to be here at this exact moment in history for a reason. Each of us is incredibly valuable, even if we sometimes think otherwise.

The second takeaway is that we get to take joy in the fact that Jesus will not only destroy death in the end but that He also wants to help us overcome our battles now. A war isn't fought in one day; it's fought over a long period of time. The battles you face in your own life fit into the big picture. Jesus wants to be in your daily life and help you overcome the obstacles and adversity you face because He loves you, He died for you, and He wants to fight for you right now. We're a part of the greatest story ever told even though the Bible was completed roughly 2,000 years ago, so we have to understand that the adversity we're facing in life isn't insignificant. We have to ask Jesus to come in and help us because we're hardwired to need help; it's ok to not do it alone.

Community in Christ

*"So we, though many, are one body in Christ,
and individually members one of another."*
Romans 12:5

The drive from my hometown to Conway, Arkansas, the city where I went to college, was about six hours long; only a fraction of it was interstate, so whenever I had to make this trip I spent a lot of time driving through small towns.

There's something that sticks out when you drive through these towns on a Sunday: all of these churches have orange road signs outside to caution passing drivers that church is going on. The traffic is so congested around these churches and there are so many people backing out of the parking lot that they had to warn the people driving by.

It's a beautiful thing to see these parking lots packed on Sundays in these small towns all through

North Louisiana and Arkansas because it's a great picture of the church that Jesus created: a community in Christ. However, the strength of churches in small towns isn't emblematic of the state of Christianity in America. Even though there are more people in the world at this point in history who have heard the Gospel, in the United States, we seem to be dragging behind. The church in America is in a weird place.

The term "church" is pretty vague. It usually refers to a building that people go to on Sundays, but when the Bible talks about the church, it's talking about everyone on earth who has given their life to Jesus. Scripture even talks about the church being Christ's bride. That's why the lessons of marriage in the New Testament also apply to Jesus and the church. For example, it talks about how men should be ready to lay down their lives for their wives just like Jesus did for the church.[1] In Revelation, it even talks about a wedding between Jesus and the church that's going to happen when Christ comes back. It says, "Let us rejoice and exult and give Him glory, for the marriage of the lamb has come, and His bride has made herself ready."[28]

We make ourselves ready by helping to bring as many people to Christ as possible which is something we can't do on our own. It has to be a team effort, and in this country, we've been doing a bad job recently.

---

[1] Ephesians 5:25

According to Pew Research, 63% of Americans don't go to church at least once a week, and, of the people who do go to church at least once a week, only 22% of them were millennials, yet 73% of Americans identify themselves as Christians.

The same study also showed that income wasn't a factor in church attendance; roughly the same percentages of people either went to church regularly or didn't in each income bracket. For example, of the people who go at least once a week, 35% made less than $30,000 per year and 18% made over $100,000 per year, and in the group of people who seldom/never go to church, 35% made less than $30,000 per year and 19% made over $100,000.

The same is true when they used education as a factor; roughly an equal percentage of people either regularly went to church or never went to church, whether they were high school dropouts or had multiple degrees. So what is it? Why is the status of churches in America dwindling, and does this paint a troubling picture of the future of faith in America?

The reality is that the church in America is in trouble. Because of this, we need to rally together if we want to turn this ship around. America is in a unique position because Christianity is so prevalent here. There aren't a lot of people who haven't heard about Jesus, but there are a ton of people who have heard about Jesus and don't want anything to do with Christians. This is one-hundred percent our fault. I can't count the number of times people have told me that the reason why they no longer go to church or lost their faith is because they felt ostracized or judged by their church when they were younger.

Between the judgmental nature of some and the boring nature of others, we as American Christians have done a horrible job of leading people to Christ. If we expect to win hearts for God and accomplish the mission to spread the gospel to every nation, we have to change our approach. Love and community is how we get people out of bed on Sundays, not lectures and judgment.

There's a story in the Gospel shows us that this isn't a new challenge. One day Jesus was in the temple when a mob of Pharisees came to Him with a woman who had been caught in the act of adultery, meaning they busted her with a man who wasn't her husband and dragged her to Jesus, naked and against her will. They pointed out that she had been caught in the act of adultery and they noted that the Old Testament law of Moses mandated that she get stoned to death, which is an absolutely horrible way to die. Whenever they were saying this, Jesus started writing in the dirt with his finger. The Bible doesn't say exactly what He wrote in the dirt, but it is the only sermon that He ever wrote down.

Some have speculated that He was writing the sins of the woman's accusers or that He was writing the names of the women that the Pharisees had slept with. Either way, the Pharisees were very embarrassed. Jesus then stood up and said one of the most famous one-liners in history: "He who is without sin, cast the first stone."[2] Then after He said that, He bent back down and kept writing in the dirt.

One by one, they all dropped their rocks and walked away. When they all left, Jesus said to her "'Woman, where are they? Has no one condemned you?' She said, 'No one, Lord' And Jesus said, 'Neither do I condemn you. Go, and from now on, sin no more.'"[3]

Now here's an important question we can get out of this: do you think that woman went home excited that she had gotten a free pass to do whatever she wanted, or do you think she was overwhelmed by the grace and forgiveness of Jesus that she not only wanted to follow him but also wanted to lead a better life? I'm willing to bet she was so moved by Jesus that she wanted to be a better person.

This is how we bring our neighbors to Christ. We can't do it by judging them and condemning them. We can only do it by loving them the way Christ loves us. Because at the end of the day we're all sinners, and we all need Jesus. No matter how much or how little we've sinned in our lives, we need God. It's not our place to put people down and to hurt them. In the eyes of God, no human is better than another regardless of the good or bad things

---

[2] Mathew 8:7
[3] Mathew 8:1-11

we may have done. Our goal should be to walk with Jesus and to go through life with each other because the best way to help people grow is to love them, encourage them, hold them accountable, and to forgive them.

Abraham Lincoln said that a house divided cannot stand, and the same applies to the church. We need each other and we need to come together. We need to be a community in Christ.

Just like the story with the woman caught in adultery, God constantly tells us how we should treat each other. Luckily for us, He also gave us a blueprint for how to build a community in Christ. Jesus spent all of His time with twelve men. He went through life with them and ministered to them for three years, so by the time Jesus left them to be in Heaven, they were ready to go out and disciple others. There are now billions of Christians in the world, and it all started with eleven guys who dedicated their lives to spreading the Gospel.

The book of Acts is an account of how they went from town to town building the early church, and it's a model for us on how to do the same thing. The formula that God lays out, the one that the apostles used, is fairly simple: discipleship and community. What this means is, for example, you would disciple your friend by talking to them about your faith, loving them, walking with them through life, teaching them about Jesus, and then after a while they'll turn around and do the same thing for some-one else and so on and so on. Then everyone gets together on Sundays, as a community, to worship God together. That's the most effective way to grow the church.

The contemporary churches who stick to this model have been very successful in recent years. The number of people who attend these churches dou-bled during the period of 2000-2016, a time period when average church attendance in the United States was falling.[4] This success is because they tend to stick to this model that's laid out in the book of Acts. They usually start out in someone's house, and through discipleship and community, they grow larger and larger over time. They also tend to heavily encourage people to get into small groups and study the Bible together during the week. When we do these things, people are much more willing to follow Jesus because they know that they'll get to be a part of a community.

Even though Christianity in America has taken a hit in the last few decades, there will always be hope as long as Christ is the head of the church. For us to get back on track and reverse the decline of faith in America, we have to get back to the blue-print that God gave us. You also don't need to be a priest or a pastor to do this. We can always spread

---

[4] Earls, Aaron. "What Does the Growth of Nondenominationalism Mean?" Facts & Trends, August 16, 2019. https://factsandtrends.net/2017/08/08/what-does-the-growth-of-nondenominationalism-mean/.

the Gospel and disciple people; it doesn't matter where we are in life or what we do. That's how we build a community in Christ.

Principles Last, Trendy Doesn't

"Trust in the LORD with all your heart and lean not on your own understanding; in all your ways submit to him, and he will make your paths straight."

Proverbs 3:5-6

I love going through college towns because you notice all of the new restaurants and stores that probably wouldn't have been popular ten years ago. A lot of trendy businesses tend to pop up in college towns because they have thousands of twenty year olds that these stores are trying to appeal to. I remember driving to College Station one summer for baseball and noticing how the entire city is built around Texas A&M; there are so many businesses there trying to appeal to the students, so it's a really trendy place. However, for every town like that, there are one or two where every building is out of style and looks out of place.

How often do you drive by a shopping center that was built in the eighties but looks horrible and tacky now? Or have your friends ever given you a hard time when they found old photos of you from back in the day? Every year, it seems, around the time of the NBA draft, people compare the outfits worn by the players to the ones worn from years past. They'll show all of these guys from the early 2000s wearing these baggy suits, and every year, without fail, someone shows the photo of a young LeBron James wearing an all-white suit when he went Number 1 overall. The reason why they do this is because baggy suits are funny to look at now but ten years ago, they were in style. If someone had shag carpets in the seventies, it looked really cool, but not many people pay to get that put in their house now.

Trendy doesn't last. The reason why it doesn't is because we have a short attention span. Humans are curious by nature and will move on to the next thing eventually, which is to say that culture is temporary, and it can lie to you.

The world around us is constantly lying and misleading us in ways not only involving trends but also sin. The reason why God tells us what to do in any situation is because He always knows what's best for us and wants us to go in the right direction.

The first four of the Ten Commandments talk about how we should conduct our relationship with

God. They tell us not to have other gods before Him, not to worship false idols, not to take the Lord's name in vain, and to honor the Sabbath. God didn't arbitrarily come up with these; they all have a specific purpose.

He tells us not to worship other gods before Him because he understands that He's the only thing that lasts forever and will never let us down. This is really the reason for the next commandment which is not to have false idols. In the 21st century, a false idol could be a career, something in a garage, a girlfriend/ boyfriend, or any blessing that God has given us that we allow to take up more space in our hearts than God himself. Those blessings can't fulfill us the way God can.

We're told not to take the Lord's name in vain, which may seem unnecessary, but God knows the key part of building any great relationship is respect. There was a study done a few years ago by a man named Dr. John Gottman where he tried to find the biggest indicators that a couple would get divorced. His claim to fame was that he could predict whether or not a couple would get a divorce with 90% accuracy, and he concluded that one of the biggest signs that a marriage would end was a lack of respect between the two.[1] God understands that contempt and disrespect undermine relationships.

---

[1] Prooyen, Eva Van. "This One Thing Is the Biggest Predictor of Divorce." The Gottman Institute, February 15, 2018. https://www.gottman.com/blog/this-one-thing-is-the-biggest-predictor-of-divorce/.

In ancient Israel, when the Jewish leaders would copy down Scripture, every time they would get to a point where they had to write down God's name, they would get a special pen and then once they were done, they would throw it away as a sign of respect. There's a certain reverence that we owe to God, and a major part of it is to not take His name in vain. We keep the Sabbath because God understands the human need for rest. He understands that life can speed up on us and that we need to slow down once a week.

What we see as rules are actually God giving us a roadmap of how to build and respect our relationship with Him.

The rest of the commandments tell us how to treat each other. We're told not to commit adultery, lie about our neighbor, or steal because trust is essential, not only to building relationships but building civilization in general. Trust is critical to everything. Think about how much of a pain it would be if you didn't trust your stock broker or if you didn't trust pilots. You'd have to drive everywhere which could get pretty inconvenient and you wouldn't have the time or resources to invest your money as efficiently as you otherwise could. God understood that trust is the main ingredient to any bond between people. It was true four thousand years ago and it's still true today.

Forbidding murder really doesn't need to be explained, but it's another example of God telling us a lot of different things with just one sentence. One obvious reason for this commandment is because murder is a horrible thing. But the other reasons God tells us not to murder are that we don't have the authority to play God, that every life is precious, and that we don't have the right to dictate someone else's life, including the decision of whether or not they get to keep it. The reason why God tells us not to covet our neighbor's stuff is because He understands how destructive jealousy is. It can ruin friendships, marriages, and it incentivizes people to do dishonest things.

The Ten Commandments weren't arbitrary rules that God made up on a whim; they were all given for a reason because God understands human behavior better than anyone, which means He knows what we have to do to have our best possible life. He gave them to us so we can all build a better world together.

Jesus took all of the 613 Old Testament laws and boiled them all down into one sentence in the New Testament: "'Love the Lord your God with all your heart and with all your soul and with all your mind.' This is the first and greatest commandment. And the second is like it: 'Love your neighbor as yourself.'..."[2]. The reason why God tells us to do anything is because He understands, better than we do, that we live in a fallen world, one governed by human nature.

---

[2] Mathew 22:37-39

Human nature tells us to get as much as we can for as little effort, so it pushes us to lie, cheat, and steal. The commandments that God gave us counteract human nature. So while culture tells us to sin, God calls us to follow Him. When our human desires tell us to be jealous of our neighbor's new car, God says to be thankful for the blessings in our own lives.

The difference between classic and trendy is that classic stands the test of time. Trendy is temporary, vain, fleeting, and so is sin. Following Christ involves something called delayed gratification: doing what is difficult now so that we can benefit later. A life for Christ gives us something much more meaningful and fulfilling than anything the world could offer. It's the same reason why marine boot camp is so difficult: because it builds toughness which comes in handy later on when they get deployed and are asked to do tough things. It's much more fun to go on a shopping spree rather than invest money into a savings account or a mutual fund, but your future self would be appreciative of you if you saved that money rather than spending it on something dumb you won't use or wear in a year. Obeying God and following Jesus is a lot like that. It's difficult and it's less comfortable than sinning, but at the end of the day God knows what's best for us long term, both in our lives and for our eternity with him.

When the world wants us to do one thing, and God wants us to do another, it will take guts to listen to God because, chances are, a lot of people around us will do what the world wants them to do, but it's always better in the long run to follow Christ. Trendy doesn't last; neither do earthly possessions or fun times. There's always a hangover, but God will never leave us or let us down. His way is always better than our own because it's higher than our own.

When the Fire Calls Our Name

*"Jesus was walking by the Sea of Galilee.
He saw two brothers. They were Simon (his
other name was Peter) and Andrew, his
brother. They were putting a net into the sea
for they were fishermen. Jesus said to them,
"Follow Me. I will make you fish for men!"
At once they left their nets and followed
Him. Going from there, Jesus saw two other
brothers. They were James and John, the
sons of Zebedee. They were sitting in a boat
with their father, mending their nets. Jesus
called them. At once they left the boat and
their father and followed Jesus."*

Matthew 4:18-22

It can be frustrating at times trying to understand
what God is saying to us. He often talks to us in a
subtle way, like when we're in the car driving to

work or when we can't fall asleep at night. But every once in a while, God is a little more obvious. Every once in a while, a fire yells as us. A long time ago, in a Middle-Eastern dessert, God talked to Moses through a burning bush to let him know that he was going to be the one to lead the Israelites out of slavery.

Imagine what it was like for Moses that day. One could assume it was a little shocking considering that Moses had spent a third of his life watching sheep after running away from Egypt. Every day of his life during that time was the same; all he did was watch sheep. He got married and had a livelihood, but for the most part his whole life was in the dessert watching sheep. Nothing about it was eventful. It's not like today where you can live out in the country but you still have Wi-Fi. This guy had nothing to do other than watch sheep for forty years, but then one night, his whole world changed.

In a shocking turn of events, Moses was watching sheep. He was taking care of his father-in-law's flock when he saw a fire. He noticed that it was a bush, but it wasn't burning up, so he walked over to check it out. When he got there, God called him by name from the bush, and Moses answered, "Here I am." As we read that story, it doesn't seem like a big deal, but imagine how freaky it would be if a fire started yelling at you. I hate horror movies and that would make me have flashbacks to middle school when my friends made me watch *Insidious*, and I would probably take off running. It takes a lot of courage just to walk up to God when He calls you out, especially when he does so using pyrotechnics.

As he was walking towards the bush, God said, "Don't come any closer." And then God told him, "Take off your sandals, for the place where you are standing is holy ground."[1] Again, this is something about the story that's a little weird. What does Moses taking off his shoes have to do with anything? Why does God have to include this detail in here? Why is He acting like that excessively clean neighbor who makes you take off your shoes when you go in their house? Even though the sandal thing is a little odd, it's actually fairly simple. God is telling Moses, in a way, to humble himself. By taking off his sandals, Moses is paying respect to the holy ground; there isn't anything in between his foot and the dirt he's standing on.

Right after the sandal comment, God introduced himself. He said "I am the God of your father, the God of Abraham, the God of Isaac and the God of Jacob."[2] And then, once God said who He was, Moses hid his face because he was scared to look at Him, as if Moses didn't know who it was before the introduction. Then God went on to explain the situation to Moses. He tells him that the Israelites have been suffering in Egypt, that it was time to get them out of there, and that Moses was going to be the one to do it.

---

[1] Exodus 3:5
[2] Exodus 3:6

That's got to be a bit of a shock. How do you go from living out in the dessert, surrounded by sheep and silence, to leading a few million enslaved people out of nation lead by an oppressive dictator? And Moses realizes this, he asks God straight up, "Who am I that I should go to Pharaoh and bring the Israelites out of Egypt?"[3]

Right here, Moses showed doubt in himself. But here's what Moses missed: God doesn't call the equipped, he equips the called. On the surface, Moses wasn't equipped to handle this. He hadn't been in a leadership role since he was a prince in Egypt forty years ago, and his closest friends were his wife, his father-in-law, and a bunch of sheep. Moses didn't think he was able to lead all of these people, and when he told God that, all God said back to him was "I'll be with you."[4]

Moses then told God that he was worried that the Jewish elders wouldn't take him seriously, to which God told him to mention that he was sent by God himself. When God told him what he was destined to do, Moses immediately said he wasn't good enough and then, right away, gave an excuse as to why he couldn't get it done.

Later on, in the next chapter, Moses gave God another excuse; he said that he wasn't eloquent, meaning he couldn't speak well. Immediately, God said, "Who gave human beings their mouths? Who

---

[3] Exodus 3:11
[4] Exodus3:12

makes them deaf or mute? Who gives them sight or makes them blind? Is it not I, the LORD?[12] Now go; I will help you speak and will teach you what to say."[5] He was basically telling Moses: I know all of this stuff, but I'm choosing you anyway. And then, Moses just comes out and says it: "Pardon your servant, Lord. Please send someone else." He was giving all of these excuses but the root issue was simple: he was terrified and he was content with where he was at in life. And frankly, why shouldn't he have been ? He was an old man who had this comfortable life away from these toxic rulers in Egypt, and now God was telling him to waltz right back into the thick of it and lead a couple million people out of bondage.

Just like Moses, it's completely natural for us to feel anxious or worried when God tells us to do something because it requires faith and that's hard. Faith means we have to let go and admit that God knows what's best for us more so than we do. And what makes it even more nerve racking is that God doesn't call us to do something big when we're ready. He calls us to do it when He's ready. Almost always, these two times don't happen simultaneously.

We're rarely ready when God calls us to enter the fight. When He calls us when we aren't ready, it takes faith on our part. In times when we feel completely lost, we have no other choice but to lean on God.

---

[5] Exodus 4:11-12

Psalms says, "Thy word is a lamp unto my feet," because faith is a one-step-at-a-time process. Our job is to move our feet; God's job is to get us in the right direction, not the other way around. We aren't supposed to know every detail of how the future is going to play out, just like how Moses had no idea what was going to ensue after he went back into Egypt.

A lot of times we want to control our destiny and get God to take out all the obstacles, but that's not how it works. Moses felt like he wasn't ready to take on this challenge, and the only reason he eventually pulled it off was because he had faith knowing that God was in his corner. When we're told by the Father to do something, it can be scary because we don't know what's going to happen. Humans are naturally scared of the unknown; that's why horror movies make stuff pop out of dark rooms.

But the reality is that we aren't scared of the unknown, we're scared of what could be in the unknown. We aren't scared of the dark; we're scared of what could be in the dark. We get terrified to say yes to God because we have no idea what lies ahead, and we have to have faith that He'll lead us in the right direction.

Earlier in the burning bush story, when God was explaining to Moses what he had to do, He asked him a simple question: "What is that in your hand?"[6] It was his shepherd's staff, which represented his life.

---

[6] Exodus 4:2

When God calls us to do something, He asks us two things. The first question is, "what's in your hand?" Meaning, what do you have to offer? Is it your career? Your talents? Your past? Your life? The truth is that it's everything. God asks us for everything we've got, regardless of whether or not we think it's enough. And in a way it's a very humbling thing because God is essentially telling us that we are good enough, even if the world tells us otherwise. He's telling us that we were made for a purpose and that we can accomplish what He calls us to do because He will always be with us.

The second thing God asks us to do is to trust him. He asks us to give up our lives and follow Him. In the New Testament, Jesus talks about picking up your cross to follow Him. A simple example happens toward the beginning of the Gospels when Jesus is picking his disciples. We can assume that Jesus had a reputation before this happened, so when He asked Peter, Andrew, James, and John to leave everything behind to follow Him, they did it no questions asked. All they did was say, "yes sir," and because of that, they eventually spread the Gospel of Jesus all over the world. It took faith for them to make that decision. It's the same concept here with Moses. He's telling him to have the faith to give up his life and do what is asked of him.

When God speaks to us, as He does for everybody in one way or another, it may be scary, but He will do things that you never could've imagined. Moses thought he was completely unqualified, but he ended up leading the Israelites out of slavery. He saved millions of lives, became one of the greatest leaders in human history, and the only reason he pulled it off was because of his faith in God. He was able to do this because he had the courage to say "yes sir."

Another thing to do when God calls us to do the impossible is to take off your sandals like Moses did. Our mission from God is holy ground; we can't separate our feet from the ground, but instead we have to humbly present ourselves to the Lord. It's amazing what we're capable of if we just have the courage to listen to God rather than fear or our own insecurities. Have faith that He'll lead you out of slavery.

Giving Your Body as a Living Sacrifice

"I appeal to you therefore, brothers, by the
mercies of God, to present your bodies as
a living sacrifice, holy and acceptable to
God, which is your spiritual worship."

Romans 12:1 ESV

Throughout my entire baseball career, I always had problems because I would constantly be worried about a dozen other things that I had no control over. It was a complete roadblock. One time, during my junior season in college, there was a weekend in particular where it seemed like nothing was going our way as a team and I was also dealing with personal issues that were affecting me on the field. And on that Saturday in Rome, Georgia, our coach walked up to me and gave me one piece of advice: play where your feet are.

At first, this sounded really weird until he explained it to me. He basically told me that you can't control what's around you, you have no idea what's going to happen tomorrow, and you have no control over what happened yesterday; you can only do your best at this current moment in time. Paul gave this same advice to the Christians in Rome, around two thousand years ago, in the beginning of Romans 12.

The first eleven chapters of the book of Romans are basically Paul making the argument for Jesus in a letter to the Jews and Gentiles in Rome, and the twelfth chapter is a summary of how to live as a follower of Christ. "Present your bodies as a living sacrifice," he says, and then he tells them, "[it] is your spiritual worship." Telling people to present their bodies as a living sacrifice sounds like something a cult leader would tell his followers. It seems really weird and vague. But, I really think the underlying message is simple. Paul is telling the people in Rome the same thing my coach told me: play where your feet are.

He's telling us to do the absolute best that we can wherever we may be in life. We should worship God every Sunday, but just as important, we should worship God with our actions Monday through Saturday. God created each of us, unlike anyone else on the planet, for a reason. We've all been given certain gifts, abilities, and adversities for a specific purpose. There has never been and will never be a person exactly like you. We can glorify God in our everyday lives with these things, and it's easier than you may think.

The first thing we have to do is recognize and acknowledge that our talents are a blessing and a gift from God. Second, we have to understand that these talents can be used to glorify God and not just to advance our careers. Third, when adversity comes our way, as it does for every man and woman that walks the earth, we have to understand that our own strength isn't enough and that God's strength can carry us over the finish line. The third one is the toughest part because it involves faith.

Relying on God's strength to carry us through is an incredibly difficult thing to do, especially if you have a Type-A personality because it involves placing your trust and your passion in the hands of someone you can't see. We may ask ourselves, "what if God doesn't come through for me?" or "what if he won't help me because what I'm doing isn't really that important?"

The answer to the first question is simple: if you ask God for something with faith and the right intentions, He will always come through for you in one way or another. I heard a story about a salesman who prayed to do $200,000 in commission for the year, which was way more than the norm. That year he gave away money as if he would make $200,000. By the end of the year, he had hit his goal of $200,000. God loves to come through for us, and if He doesn't come through for us in the way that we may have hoped, it ends up being a bigger blessing than what we prayed for originally.

One of Garth Brooks' greatest hits is about how God's greatest gifts are unanswered prayers, and the reason this song was such a huge hit is because it resonated with so many people. Everyone knows the feeling of asking God for something and not getting a yes, but the good news is that God blesses us even when we don't get a yes.

Whenever we pray for something, God answers in one of three ways: yes, not yet, or "I have something better in mind." Getting the yes is amazing, but getting the other two require faith, and that's always a little more difficult. Faith means acknowledging that God's way is always better than our own and that He wants what's best for us when He answers our prayers in one of those three ways. If we face adversity and ask God for his strength to carry us through, He will always show up for us. If you stay faithful and do the right thing over and over, eventually, God will show up and show off.

There's an encouraging answer to the question, "what if God won't help me because what I'm doing isn't really that important?"

In one of Jesus' most famous miracles, he takes five loaves of bread and three fish and feeds five thousand men, which was actually way more than five thousand people because the phrase "five thousand men" is literal. They only counted the men which means there were probably around ten thousand people in total. Whenever we hear that story, the common message is that Jesus comes through for us in miraculous ways, but one element that we don't often talk about is the boy who gave him the bread and the fish.

In John Chapter 6, whenever they were faced with the task of feeding these people, Peter says, "two hundred denarii worth of bread would not be enough for each of them to get a little."[1] For reference, a denarii was the equivalent of one day's pay for a skilled laborer. In today's terms, if we took the average wage for a welder in the United States and multiplied it over a 10-hour day then multiplied that over a period of 200 days, the cost to feed this crowd would be $54,000.[2,3] So we know that it would've cost a fortune to feed these people and then right afterwards, two verses later, Peter's brother Andrew said, "There is a boy here who has five barley loaves and two fish, but what are they for so many?"

Once Jesus saw the boy with the food, He has one of the most famous "I got this" moments in history when He said, "have the people sit down." And then we know what happened next; Jesus takes five loaves and two fishes and feeds close to ten thousand

[1] John 6:7
[2] https://www1.salary.com/Welder-III-hourly-wages.html
[3] Joseph. "How Much Was a Denarius Worth in Jesus' Day Compared to Today?" Study Bible Q&A, November 19, 2011. http://ask.study-bible.info/301/how-much-was-a-denarius-worth-in-jesus-day-compared-to-today.

people. The Bible even says that there were even a bunch of leftovers.

Think about how cool of an experience that was for that little boy. I imagine he went home that night and told his parents, "You won't believe what happened to me today" or several decades later when he was an old man, he sat his grandchildren on his lap and told them the story about the time a guy named Jesus fed 10,000 people with his lunch. This kid didn't have much to offer, but he gave it up to Jesus when he was asked to, and because of that small act of obedience, he's part of a story that's been told for 2,000 years and he got to be part of a blessing to 10,000 people. Sometimes we may think that we don't have much to offer, or we may think that what we do isn't important enough for God to use us, but don't be discouraged. If we're willing to offer up what we have, God will do things with our lives that we never thought were possible.

When Winston Churchill became Prime Minister of England in 1940, a time when the nation was scared to death because of imminent invasion from Nazi Germany. In his first speech to Parliament, he said, "I have nothing to offer but blood, toil, tears, and sweat." He went on to rally the British people to fight on in the face of tyranny and, as we all know, the allies came out on top. A lot of credit for the victory in World War II can be given to Winston Churchill because, due to his refusal to surrender to

Hitler in 1940, the German army had to fight a two front war against the West and against the Soviets on the east and the American military was able to launch offensives from England throughout the entire war. All of this happened after Prime Minister Churchill humbly told the British people that he had nothing to give them except for everything he had. If we approach God with this same humility and bravery, He will do miracles in our lives.

You are always good enough for God to use you. As a matter of fact, you are the only person in history that can live out the purpose that God has for you. But when you feel overwhelmed, play where your feet are. Offer what you have as a sacrifice to God. If you're an athlete, give everything you have, play the game with faith, and take joy in the sport God has blessed you with the ability to play.

If you work in an office, take a coworker out to lunch, ask them if they're struggling with anything, and offer to help out if you can. Love the people around you, make real friendships, and share the Gospel with them. Even if you feel like you're in a valley right now or that the world has beaten you down, your circumstance can be used to glorify Christ; ask God what he wants you to do, and for the love of God, don't ever give up.

The Whisper of a Lady Bug

"Therefore I tell you, do not be anxious about your life, what you will eat or what you will drink, nor about your body, what you will put on. Is not life more than food, and the body more than clothing? Look at the birds of the air: they neither sow nor reap nor gather into barns, and yet your heavenly Father feeds them. Are you not of more value than they? And which of you by being anxious can add a single hour to his span of life? And why are you anxious about clothing? Consider the lilies of the field, how they grow: they neither toil nor spin, yet I tell you, even Solomon in all his glory was not arrayed like one of these. But if God so clothes the grass of the field, which today is alive and tomorrow is thrown into the oven, will he not much

*more clothe you, O you of little faith?
Therefore do not be anxious, saying, 'What
shall we eat?' or 'What shall we drink?' or
'What shall we wear?' For the Gentiles
seek after all these things, and your
heavenly Father knows that you need them
all. But seek first the kingdom of God and
his righteousness, and all these things will
be added to you."*

- Matthew 6:25-33

I can still remember the day God spoke to me with
the same clarity as a flashing neon light in the sky.
The trip down I-20 west can get boring, so the time
was usually passed with my thoughts and the radio,
and on that day, I had a lot to think about. Fifteen
months earlier, on August 6th, 2014, I was eating a
second lunch getting ready for the second football
practice of the day on the Wednesday of a "two-a-
day week." It was the fall of my senior year of high
school. With the TV on, I could hear the garage
door open and close which was a signal that my
mom was home.

When she walked in the house I could sense
there was something wrong and it became clear
when she quickly walked over to me, avoiding eye
contact, and said, "Sid was complaining about some
pain in his leg, they went to the doctor to check on
it, and the doctor found a mass on his knee. They

don't know if its benign or malignant, but I want you to be prepared for whatever happens." Sid was my cousin from Birmingham, AL who, although he was three years younger than me, he was like my brother. Roughly five hours later after I had returned from the most distracted practice of my life, I was sitting on the floor of my room anxiously waiting for the news. Then suddenly, the door swung open and my mom told me, "It's cancer," as she immediately began to sob.

Most people would agree that seeing your own mother crying is one of the most disheartening and discouraging things to be a part of, and this was definitely not an exception. Because of that, I decided it was my duty to be an emotional rock. I realized that it was time for me to grow up and be a man. I wasn't going to let myself show pain. Of course that went out the window the next day when Sid texted me and told me he was going to win and be closer to God as a result of that victory. In that moment, I felt this wave of fear and emotion knock me down and in my kitchen; I started to sob like my mom did the night before.

What followed was a fifteen-month emotional roller coaster. For over a year after the diagnosis, into the fall of 2015, Sid battled osteosarcoma, a rare form of bone cancer. Several months beforehand, when it had become clear that the cancer had spread into his lungs and didn't show any signs of regression, it was obvious that he wasn't going to make it. In spite of the aggressive nature of the disease, that fall, Sid became a national star.

He had inspired hundreds of thousands of people in Alabama with his courage. People were so moved that a cancer-stricken teenager could go on living his life as if nothing was wrong. It made people realize that adversity didn't matter and that what did matter was how we respond to it. His story eventually stretched much further than his community, and ironically it was because of the dynamics at play inside of his community.

Sid and his family lived in Birmingham, Alabama but the rest of our family lives in south Louisiana. Sid's family and their Cajun roots led them to be lifelong LSU fans. Their purple and gold blood made life interesting in Birmingham which is filled with a Crimson Tide army and a few Auburn fans mixed in. But despite the southern rivalry at play, in support for Sid, every mailbox on his street was decorated with purple and gold balloons when he came back from the hospital one day, which was just the beginning. People started to wear purple and gold in solidarity with Sid, and everyday at 4:00 pm, the whole community would come together to pray for him.

Sid had captured the hearts of north Alabama but soon afterward, he captured the heart of the nation. One day, Les Miles, the head football coach at LSU, heard about Sid's fight and his love for the

Tigers, and he decided to call him. The call was one of the highlights of Sid's life; they talked about the upcoming matchup, made fun of Nick Saban, and then Coach Miles told him something that none of us will ever forget. Through that grainy, speaker phone sound, we could hear the voice of the coach say to him, "When you get to heaven, save me a spot." This immediately caught people's attention, and that night on Sports Center, Scott Van Pelt told a national audience about Les Miles telling my cousin Sid to save him a spot in Heaven.

Soon there afterward, Sid and the coach struck up a friendship, which involved getting invited to be coach Miles' personal guest at the Auburn game in Tiger Stadium. That day was the greatest day of his life. Sid got to tour the locker room, the facilities, and right before the team ran out onto the field, Les Miles came up to him, hugged him, and whispered into his ear. We didn't know what he said until much later; Coach Miles wanted that to be a personal moment between Sid and him. Eventually, after his passing, we found out that Les told him that he loved him.

Twenty-eight days later, once I had gotten home from college for the weekend, my mom told me that Sid was in tough shape; they were scared he wouldn't make it until the morning, and that we were going to get up early the next morning to make the seven-hour drive to Birmingham while praying we get there in time. Fortunately, we did. I'll never forget the hopeless feeling I got when we walked into his hospital room and there was a priest performing last rites on him; that was the moment when I couldn't be in denial anymore and had to confront the fact that he was dying.

What was interesting about that situation was the fact that Sid grew up going to a non-denominational church every week and could probably count on one hand the times he's heard a Catholic priest speak. My grandmother, on the other hand, was very Catholic and the sight of Sid receiving the sacrament of Anointing of the Sick was a huge source of peace for her. Especially since no one knew the priest was coming, it was almost like divine intervention placed the priest on the eighth floor, quarterback tower, of Birmingham Children's hospital at the exact time we arrived there with my devoutly Catholic grandmother.

That night, per Sid's request, his older brother and I slept with him in his hospital room and we almost had heart attacks because Sid thought it was a great idea to unhook a bunch of wires, get out of bed, and walk to the bathroom which lead to a chorus of monitors and brought in a team of sprinting nurses.

The next day, Sid was taken home on hospice care. We stayed with him at his house for a couple of more nights and then we all returned the next weekend to spend more time with him. The next weekend was more relaxed; Sid was feeling better, was in good spirits, and our whole family was together, just like old times. It's funny how God will use adversity and tragedy to show us how blessed we are. We left Birmingham, after that weekend, in peace. We had seen all of the love Sid had from his friends and family; we saw the impromptu candlelight vigil his classmates put on outside of his house; we got to be together as a family; and we got to pray together.

We all understood what was about to happen, but we knew where he was headed and we got to see, up close, the impact that he had on his community. Most importantly, we got to see how many people became closer to Christ as a result of Sid's courage and his faith.

At the end of that weekend, I made the five-hour trek back to Louisiana Tech, where I went to school at the time. The whole drive was a rotation between feelings of fear, sadness, anxiety, nostalgia, and peace. I was scared of what life was going to be like after he died, sad because I knew we were about to lose him, anxious because we had no idea when it was going to happen, and nostalgic thinking of the memories we had. Even though there were all of those negative emotions, there was a feeling of peace knowing that Jesus went to the cross so that we could have eternal life with Him after we left this earth.

Five days later, I was told that we were close to the end. Right then, I called my cousin Sid to tell him how much I loved him. Unfortunately, he had lost his ability to speak so they put me on speaker phone because there were several people in his room at the time. I talked to him for about five minutes, prayed with him and everyone in his room, told him I loved him one more time, said goodbye, and then hung up. This was the last time we spoke. The next morning, on Saturday October 31st, 2015, at 7:23 am Sid left us to be with Jesus.

A few days later we drove back up to Birmingham for the funeral, just like we had the two weekends before. That Wednesday evening was the visitation for family and close friends and the next morning was the burial service. The visitation turned out to be a lot more lighthearted than one would expect, which is no surprise for the people that knew him well; formality was not his calling card.

The most impactful part of that night was a simple story Sid's mom (my aunt) told me. When she knew his time was getting short, she went into his room and asked a simple favor; she told him that when he got to heaven, she wanted a sign so she knew he was ok. Originally, as a joke, he said, "Sure, I'll send you a screaming Chinese baby." We all thought that was funny, but when she asked him to be serious, he told her he'd send a lady bug. This was weird because all of this happened in mid-late

October which isn't necessarily the peak season for lady bugs, but nevertheless, he decided that a lady bug would be the right message.

The next morning, we all met up at the funeral home to get ready for the burial service. When we got to the cemetery, we noticed that we would have to carry the casket up and over a little hill. This almost caused an incident because all the pall bearers were wearing dress shoes, we weren't all the same height so this casket wasn't even close to balanced, and all of the pall bearers were all younger than 21. None of us were used to wearing dress shoes often, and we didn't realize how easy it is to slip when you walk on grass with those things. Fortunately, we didn't drop the casket even though we came close twice. Immediately after we set it down, his friend Wilson looked at me and jokingly said, "Thank God he was ninety pounds when he died," and we both laughed because if he were a heavier guy, we would've definitely slipped and that would not have been a hallmark moment.

After we set the casket down, the graveside service started and a few of us told stories about Sid and talked about his life. The pastor prayed for all of us, and we wrapped it up. Right near the end of the service, a lady bug landed on the purple and gold striped tie of Sid's best friend, Grayson. He was the first one. The day after Sid died, a few days earlier, there was a swarm of lady bugs in his church, but Grayson was the first individual to get one. After that, one by one, lady bugs started randomly appearing to people that were close to Sid. Later that day, there was a memorial service that was open to the public, thousands attended. There was a gap of a couple hours between the burial service and the memorial, so there was a small lunch for the guests of the burial service at the church before the larger memorial started. In that reception room, there were these big, twelve foot windows and on the outside of them, there were dozens of lady bugs.

The memorial service was like a scene out of a movie. There were hundreds, if not thousands of people in this massive church. Three people gave eulogies: Sid's father; his older friend and mentor, Trey; and a close family friend. Each of these three represented a different group of people in the story: Sid's family, Sid's friends, and Sid's community. After they were finished, the head pastor of the church, a man named Chris Hodges, said a few words. I remember two parts of his sermon.

The first was when he mentioned that Sid died on Halloween, saying how funny it was that his faith in Christ inspired so many people and that he passed away on the day when we mock death: a great representation of Christ's victory over death at the cross. When he said that, the place broke out in applause.

The second was a story Chris told. He was sitting on a plane pretending to be asleep so he didn't have to talk to the person next to him, when this outgoing guy sits down and starts to make conversation. Eventually, the man tells pastor Chris that he was Jewish and was making the trip back home after the funeral of his best friend. The man confided in the pastor about how sad he was that he would never see his best friend again and asked if there was any way he could have hope. When Pastor Chris got to this point in the story, I remember him telling all of us "the ball was teed up for me, if you can't hit that, you can't play," which got a lot of laughs. He told the man about Jesus and what His death and resurrection meant for us. Because Pastor Chris told the man about Jesus, he had hope and joy in knowing that he could see his friend again.

That story reminded a city and a family in mourning that, although it's painful for us, death has lost its sting. He helped us remember that this pain is temporary and because Christ died and resurrected for us; we would all be able to see Sid's smiling face again, just like that man and will be able to see his friend.

The funeral was on Thursday, and afterwards, at the reception, my cousin Andy, Sid's older brother, asked me to stay a few extra days so we could go to Tuscaloosa for the LSU vs. Alabama game that Saturday night and go backstage for College Gameday that Saturday morning, and I agreed because I couldn't think of a better way to honor Sid's memory. The whole day was incredible even though the tigers lost because we got to meet the Gameday crew: some of Sid's favorite people in the world.

The next morning, even though it was tough to do so, it was time to make the five hour trip down I-20 to go back to Louisiana Tech. I hadn't been in class for a week because of the funeral services, so I had to head back. I lingered a little bit because I wasn't quite ready to get back to reality. Regardless, it was time to go, so I got all of my bags packed, loaded up my truck, hugged everyone goodbye, and drove off.

The drive to Ruston, Louisiana from Birmingham is relatively easy; you just get on I-20, head west for a few hours, and you're there. But that drive was the definition of an emotional rollercoaster; I had a few laughs when I remembered the funny things Sid had said and done during his life and I had a few tears. But more than anything, that day hurt. I was even so depressed at one point that I asked God to send a car across the median and hit me head-on so I didn't have to deal with the pain anymore. That moment was my rock bottom.

In the three months leading up to that day, I was dumped; I left home; I was cut by the baseball team at Louisiana Tech, which led me to transfer schools; and my cousin Sid, one of my favorite people on the planet, passed away. It's interesting: people always talk about never giving up, but a lot of times we neglect how difficult perseverance is. Often times, we romanticize quitting, and we think about how easy everything would be if we just rang the bell and walked home. Sometimes we ask God to end the pain.

On that day, I begged God to make the pain go away. I couldn't imagine a scenario where things get better for me. When I had gotten to my lowest point, a lady bug appeared out of nowhere on the inside of my truck's driver side window. I've often told people this was the single happiest moment in my life because in that second, God not only told me that Sid was ok, but he also told me that I was going to be ok. God took me at my lowest point and immediately gave me true happiness. There are moments when we want nothing more that to throw in the towel. We feel completely powerless. In those times, God shows His glory through us.

Before Jesus was arrested He went up to the Mount of Olives to be alone and pray. Being God, He knew exactly what was about to happen to Him. He completely understood the pain He was about to experience. He begged the father to stop it before it happened, saying "Father, if you are willing, please take this cup of suffering away from me, yet I want your will be done, not mine."[1] God knew the higher purpose for Christ's suffering, so He allowed it to happen.

---

[1] Luke 22:42

How many times have you or I begged God to take away our hardship? How often do we want nothing more than for adversity to be gone? God never fails to use our pain for His glory. Even though Jesus endured arguably the worst pain that has ever been endured by a human being, it was for the salvation of every single person that has ever lived; it was for every child of God.

Whether it's a breakup, a layoff, financial problems, or trouble at home, pain is necessary for growth. In the times when we ask God to take this cup from us and take our suffering away, we have to remember the greater plan, and although it may be difficult; we have to keep fighting and don't forget that God always uses our pain for His glory. There is always light at the end of a tunnel and a mountain when we get out of the valley. In the first chapter of Leonard Mlodinow's book, *The Drunkard's Walk*, he says, "successful people in every field are almost universally members of the same set: the set of people who do not give up."[2]

God sent me a lady bug to tell me that everything was going to be ok. I don't know how God will tell you the same thing, but He will. He holds you in the palm of His hand and has a higher plan for you. When Sid was diagnosed, thousands of people started wearing lime green wristbands to show support. On one side was a simple message:

[2] Mlodinow, Leonard. *The Drunkards Walk: How Randomness Rules Our Lives.* New York: Pantheon Books, 2009.

"Pray for Sid." On the other side was the promise God made to Jeremiah: "'For I know the plans I have for you,' declares the Lord, 'plans to prosper you and not to harm you, plans to give you hope and a future.'"[3]

It may not feel like it, and you may be going through a lot of pain, but God always wants to lift you up. That's the goal in the end. That day, God gave me the greatest lesson I have ever learned in my life, and He didn't do it with writing in the sky or by yelling at me, He whispered to me while I was on the highway. He told me that not only was Sid okay but that I was going to be okay.

In Kings 19:12, it says that "after the earthquake there was a fire, but the Lord was not in the fire. And after the fire there was a voice, a soft whisper." The months leading up to that moment made me feel as if the world was on fire, but after all of it, God whispered to me and reminded me that He was still in control.

At my lowest point, God still was able to remind me that I'm completely in the palm of His hand, and that every ounce of pain is completely meaningful; there was no point in worrying about everything or trying to fight through this on my own because all I had to do was trust in Christ and have faith knowing He can take care of the rest.

---

[3] Jeremiah 29:11 (NIV)

CPSIA information can be obtained
at www.ICGtesting.com
Printed in the USA
LVHW081420130520
655518LV00019B/1675

9 781646 107681